Untapped Wealth Discovered

Some of the safest markets you will ever find.
A simple guide as to how you can discover those safe, but
hidden, niche and untapped markets that will enable you to
generate real income for as long as you require.
Written by
Jeff N Marquis and Kerry J Harrison
May 2005
Special Business Needs Consultants
Published by
<u>www.Untappedwealth.com</u>
Copyright May 2005
All rights reserved by Sterling Creations

To order additional copies, please contact us.
BookSurge, LLC
www.booksurge.com
1-866-308-6235
orders@booksurge.com

Untapped Wealth Discovered

Written by Jeff N Marquis and Kerry J Harrison

Sterling Creations
2005

Untapped Wealth Discovered

TABLE OF CONTENTS

Jeff and Kerry would like to dedicate their book to their many clients who have encouraged them to write a revised follow-up to "Untapped Wealth", written by Kerry Harrison in December 2002. "Untapped Wealth" was Kerry's first book and because of the overwhelmingly positive feedback from both her readers and clients she decided to team up with Jeff Marquis to write "Untapped Wealth Discovered." Kerry and Jeff would also like to thank their families and make special mention of two of their friends Linda and Andy. "Thank you both for your support, suggestions, and editorial expertise."

We would also like to give a special thank you to Vanessa King, our graphic artist and liaison with the publisher. Vanessa has contributed her creative efforts in the design of the cover for our book and we are very appreciative of her contribution.

INTRODUCTION

In 2002 Kerry Harrison wrote her very first book "Untapped Wealth" and the book became a best seller. Sales of Kerry's book started off slowly, but very soon things began to happen for this author. Sales began to increase markedly and by the end of 2004 Kerry had sold just over 10,000 books. A remarkable feat by a remarkable author!

Despite this success, Kerry is not satisfied to simply sit back and watch her book continue to sell. Because of this, she has teamed up with her colleague Jeff Marquis to write a revised version of "Untapped Wealth" which they have titled "Untapped Wealth Discovered." Jeff has brought a whole new dimension to this book and these two authors have decided to share their in-depth knowledge and experience with their readers. They have been special needs business consultants for over 20 years and they have worked with hundreds of clients to show them how they can become financially successful by taking advantage of markets that are global, untapped, undiscovered, hidden, and niche. In addition, they have provided their clients with strategies that help them stay ahead of their competition.

This book does not contain get rich quick schemes, but it does contain proven strategies and vital information that will help you to discover untapped wealth and untapped markets before your competition. In addition, the markets discussed in this book are probably the safest that you will ever find. Buzz words will be used to help you remember things more easily. By the time you have finished reading this book you will have enough information in your hands to help you become successful business persons, choose the right type of career that will make you high income earners, and be able to become one of those highly sought after experts that the American and other governments are desperately seeking. Such is the demand for these types of experts and their expertise that all of these governments are willing to pay seven figure annual incomes to anyone who can provide the right type of knowledge, service, and products.

When Jeff and Kerry are not writing books and articles they divide their time between being highly paid consultants to the American government, large corporations, and entrepreneurs, and giving motivational speeches across North America, as well as in Britain and Europe. At this point, it is time to turn things over to Jeff and Kerry as they introduce their chapters and continue on.

In chapter one, we will discuss the meaning of untapped markets and untapped wealth and give you some guidelines as to how you can go about finding other niche, hidden, and undiscovered markets that will help you to become financially successful.

In chapter two we will introduce you to one of the most powerful global markets that you will ever find. According to most business experts, this market is probably one of the most financially influential at the present time and it is estimated that it will continue to be so for a very long time to come because this particular global market will continue to be made up of more and more financially successful consumers.

In chapter three we will introduce you to another large

and untapped global market that is growing very rapidly. The demands from the consumers of this market are threatening to get out of hand and the American government along with other world governments is becoming alarmed because they are hard pressed to meet the demands of these particular consumers.

In chapter four we will introduce you to yet another global market that is quickly becoming influential around the world. The consumer demand of this market is growing rapidly and again the experts are saying that this market has the potential to be around for a very long time. In addition, there are countless opportunities for businesses to make handsome profits.

In chapter five we will introduce you to the fourth untapped global market that is also growing rapidly and is expected to be around for a very long time. This market is lucrative, filled with consumer demands, and short on supply. It presents a great opportunity for you to cash in.

In chapter six we will present you with a number of businesses that can bring you great success and we will show you how you can get a leg up on your competition.

In chapter seven we will show you what types of careers can bring you financial success.

In chapter eight we will do a wrap up and give you ways to remember some of the more important points that we have covered.

In chapter nine we will present you with some real business cases that we have chosen from among our more successful clients.

PART ONE
DISCOVERIES OF UNTAPPED WEALTH

CHAPTER ONE
UNTAPPED WEALTH AND
UNTAPPED MARKETS
HOW YOU CAN GET A BIG
HEAD START

So many persons these days are caught up in seeking their financial pot of gold and many of them are turning to unproven, make-money-fast schemes in order to get rich, but as we know, over 90% of these so-called schemes are nothing more than smoke screens. It concerns us that instead of taking the logical approach most persons are allowing themselves to be taken in by the promise of getting rich quickly. In so doing, many of them end up losing their hard earned savings, rather than making any sort of decent income.

As special needs business consultants, we have spent over 20 years working with businesses of all sizes as well as entrepreneurs. Time and time again we have had to rescue both businesses and individuals from the jaws of failure and bankruptcy because they were taken in by some sort of get-rich-quick scheme. We have been advocating our strategies throughout our careers and are happy to report that those who have chosen to follow our recipes for success have been enjoying solid, handsome profits. Whereas many financial advisers and business consultants regularly steer their clients towards volatile stock markets, our approach is to show you where to find those global untapped markets that can bring you wealth. There are lots of markets out there made up of seeming opportunities that promote rising consumer growth and increasing demand for goods and services for a short time, but in reality these markets do not possess durability. In fact many of these markets cease to exist after about five years and then many investors and businesses are left with only the shirts on their backs.

Our simple approach is to lead you to those markets that are still relatively untapped where growth will continue for a very long time. These markets are made up of consumers who will be around for years to come and their income earning power will continue to grow. We are not talking about markets that depend solely on financial investments. We are talking about markets that will naturally continue to grow both in demand and consumer size because of basic geographic, social, demographic, and natural shifts and changes in global societies. The objective of our book is to introduce you to four of the world's largest untapped markets and to show you how to make the most of them. We are going to help you discover wealth in global markets that are untapped, undiscovered, niche, and hidden. Our aim is to show you how to successfully race ahead of your competition into these markets, which are above all, some of the safest any investor could ever hope to find.

We have been promoting our strategies for over 20 years and we can tell you that on average, our corporate and business clients experience anywhere from a 10% to 40% growth annually due in large part to our strategies. We continue to help entrepreneurs to find their financial successes. We help individuals to develop side businesses and second careers and we also help college and university graduates to choose careers that will help them to become high-income earners.

Of course our strategies are not for everyone, but if you are truly serious about wanting to find those large pockets of untapped wealth then this book is for you. If you are having difficulty finding those markets where demand is way ahead of supply, or a market where competition is not too strong, this book is for you. If you are not having any luck finding those markets where consumer growth is expanding on a continuous basis, you need to read this book. If you want to earn safe income or make safe investments, read this book before you do anything else. Believe it or not, the four global markets that we are going to introduce you to are markets that will never be affected by inflation or deflation. These untapped global markets are going to be around for a long time but you need to take advantage of their relatively untapped wealth before your competition hears about them.

Before introducing our strategies and those four untapped global markets to you, we want to ensure that you are indeed ready to start looking for untapped wealth. As mentioned before, our strategies are not based on foolhardy schemes but rather on cold hard facts and very durable markets and in order for them to work for you; you need to be sure that you are ready and willing to make certain changes in your life. No one can expect to earn new or additional income without having to make some sort of sacrifice or changes in their life. Even in the case of those foolhardy get-rich-quick schemes one often has to give up lots of time and hard earned savings in order to get something in return. This is not the case with our approach.

We are going to start by giving you a list of questions to consider and we guarantee that these questions will help you to make up your mind whether or not you are ready and willing to start looking for that untapped wealth. You see, we are not asking you to invest a single dime! All we're asking is for you to take a few minutes to consider the following list of questions and we are sure that these next few minutes will prove to be very crucial to you. These questions are designed to help you decide whether or not you are ready or interested in discovering untapped wealth and they are categorized so that you can choose the category that best describes your present situation. In addition, they will give you an opportunity to examine your present financial and employment situations and you may find that, whereas before you may not have been ready to change jobs or careers for whatever reasons, the time has come for you to re-evaluate your position. So without further ado, please take a few minutes to answer the following questions and then we will help you to evaluate your answers.

The following list of questions is meant for those who are presently employed.

Are you tired of working for someone else?

Are you tired of not being recognized by your boss or your colleagues for your efforts?

Are you tired of having to fight the long hours of traffic on a daily basis to and from work?

Do you feel that your take home earnings are simply not enough to cover your basic household expenses?

Are you constantly worrying about how you will have enough income to retire comfortably?

Do you feel that your career is stalled and has nowhere to go?

Are you frustrated at work because your boss refuses to give you more responsibilities?

Would you like to become your own boss?

Are you looking for either a career change or seeking a new job?

Are you concerned that you may soon be laid off or down sized because of present economic conditions?

Do you feel that your job may be in jeopardy because you no longer possess the skills that your company is looking for?

How to evaluate your answers:

Here is how to evaluate your answers:

1 to 3 "yes" answers – you are not ready to seek untapped wealth in untapped markets.

4 to 7 "yes" answers – you should be thinking about those untapped markets that contain untapped wealth.

8 to 12 "yes" answers – it's time for you to start looking for untapped wealth in untapped markets.

The following list of questions is meant for those who are either retired or about to retire.

Do you feel financially secure at the present time?

Do you think that your savings will be enough to keep you comfortable for the rest of your life?

Do you feel that you will need to find ways to boost your income because your present savings may not be enough to keep you going?

Will you be able to continue your present life style now that your employment days are ended or coming to an end?

Are you worried about being able to support your kids in college now that you are either retired or going to retire soon?

Are you interested in finding a second career now that you are retired or when you retire?

Are you interested in investing some of your savings but you don't really know how to go about doing it?

Are you looking for those hard-to-find, safe investments?

Are you interested in becoming an entrepreneur?

Are you concerned that you may not be able to cover unexpected emergencies such as medical expenses because you may not be able to afford it?

Here is how to evaluate your answers:

1 to 4 "yes" answers – you are not ready to seek untapped wealth in untapped markets.

5 to 7 "yes" answers – you should be thinking about those untapped markets that contain untapped wealth.

8 to 10 "yes" answers – it's time for you to start looking for untapped wealth in untapped markets.

The following questions are meant for both college and university students.

Are you unsure as to which career path would be best for you?

Is a high income career top priority for you?

Is a satisfactory career top priority for you?

Are you having difficulty finding ways to finance yourself through college or university?

Are you having difficulty finding a job to help you pay your tuition?

Are you having problems finding a summer job to help pay the bills?

Do you feel that your college or university degree may not be enough to help you find a decent paying job?

Do you feel that the career you have chosen may not be the right one because the market already has too many persons with similar qualifications?

Do you feel that there may not be a demand for the career you have chosen?

Is the career path you have chosen your number one choice?

Do you feel that your guidance counselor has done a good job at helping you to choose your career path?

Do you feel that you have enough information at hand to help you choose the most suitable career for yourself?

Here is how to evaluate your answers:

1 to 4 "yes" answers – you are not ready to seek untapped wealth in untapped markets.

5 to 8 "yes" answers – you should be thinking about those untapped markets that contain untapped wealth.

9 to 12 "yes" answers – it's time for you to start looking for untapped wealth in untapped markets.

If you own a small or medium sized business or you are an entrepreneur, these questions are for you.

Are you having difficulty attracting new customers?

Have your profits been stagnant or on the decline for the past three years?

Have your costs been rising for the past three years?

Are you having difficulty keeping your costs under control?

Are you looking for new ways to expand your business?

Are your customers constantly complaining that they have difficulty accessing your website?

Are your customers happy with the information that you provide on your website?

Do your customers think that your business location is a convenient one?

Are your customers satisfied with the layout of your displays?

Are your customers generally satisfied with your services and/or products?

Are your customers happy with your customer support services?

Are your customers happy with your hours of business?

Here is how to evaluate your answers:

1 to 3 "yes" answers – you are not ready to seek untapped wealth in untapped markets.

4 to 7 "yes" answers – you should be thinking about those untapped markets that contain untapped wealth.

8 to 12 "yes" answers – it's time for you to start looking for untapped wealth in untapped markets.

This final list of questions is meant for those who are thinking of becoming entrepreneurs.

Are you thinking about becoming an entrepreneur, perhaps because you have just lost your job, but don't quite know where to start?

Do you feel that if you became an entrepreneur it would help you to pay off your bills more quickly?

Would you like to become an entrepreneur so that you could have a second career upon retirement, in an environment less stressful than at an office?

Are you thinking about entrepreneurship because it would enable you to become your own boss?

Would you like to become an entrepreneur because you have been at home for a while and are afraid to seek a full-time job?

Would you like to become an entrepreneur because you feel that you have either a service or product to offer?

Do you feel that by becoming an entrepreneur you will be able to write off some of your expenses at home?

Do you think that if you became an entrepreneur you would be able to spend more time with your family?

Do you feel that if you became an entrepreneur you would be able to make more money than if you were to work for a company?

Here is how to evaluate your answers:

1 to 5 "yes" answers – you are not ready to seek untapped wealth in untapped markets.

6 to 8 "yes" answers – you should be thinking about those untapped markets that contain untapped wealth.

9 to 12 "yes" answers – it's time for you to start looking for untapped wealth in untapped markets.

We developed these evaluations with the assistance of feedback from many of our clients along with the input from several business consultants and psychologists and we have had an over 95% satisfaction rating on the contents of these evaluations. If you were hesitant on an answer to any of the questions in the category that you chose then it is time for you to determine the answer. It is paramount that you answer all of the questions in your chosen category in order for these evaluations to work for you. Of course, some of you may feel that you fit into more than one category and that's okay. The crucial factor here is for you to determine whether or not you are ready to embark on a venture as important as this. Your level of readiness and frame of mind will go a very long way in determining your ultimate success. Believe it or not, one way for you to get an edge over your competitors is for you to be mentally ready. Half-heartedness is simply not going to cut it when it comes to beating your competitors.

WELCOME TO THE FOUR LARGEST GLOBAL MARKETS

These four global markets will be discussed in much more detail in subsequent chapters but we are going to whet your appetite by providing you with some very important stats.

Our first market is the single largest global market around at the present time. It is made up of two segments and within each of these segments there are sub segments. However, there is an overlap of segments as several consumers can be classified as belonging to both segments.

In 2002 one of the segments contained approximately 750 million global consumers and 55 million of these consumers were Americans. It is estimated that globally this segment has an annual average consumer growth of about 10% and an annual average income growth of about 15%. In addition, the annual income for the American consumers of this segment in 2002 was estimated to be about one trillion dollars and they spent about 4.3 billion dollars on technology.

These stats are from **Fortune 500** and **The New York Times**.

One of these sub segments presently consists of 42 million global consumers and the World Health Organization estimates that the size of this sub segment may be as high as 76 million by the year 2020.

The second segment of this market is made up of consumers who are probably going to be the most financially influential for at least the next 25 years. Such is their prominence and financial power that by the year 2010 it is estimated that they will make up about 60% of North America's population and own about 70% of banking assets in North America.

Both the American government and several world renowned business experts are forecasting that this particular global market will continue to grow both in size and income for at least the next 20 years and other world governments are in agreement. In addition, demand is growing at an alarming rate, supply is lagging behind, and many companies are not yet aware as to how to go about taking advantage of this relatively untapped market. You are probably wondering why this is. The answer is very simple; so simple in fact, that when we explain it to you, you will probably not believe us at first. We can assure you, however, that the answer is the key to your ability to race ahead of your competition into this market.

The general consensus among the experts and world governments including the United States is that most businesses fail to understand the pulse of this market and consequently they fail to realize the potential for tapping into untapped wealth. They have not taken the time to analyze and develop the appropriate strategies because they have failed to realize that this market contains segments that are further divided into sub segments and instead of breaking down this very huge market into logical pieces they try to see only the entire picture. As a result they miss the boat completely. In addition, many of your potential competitors are not even taking the time to get to know their potential customers, learn about their demands, understand what they are demanding, and develop strategies to fulfill these demands.

In short, your potential competitors are continually ignoring the basic **WWWH** concepts.

(**W**ho are the consumers, **W**hat are they demanding, **W**hy are they making these demands, and **H**ow can businesses fulfill these demands)

Here is the 20 year forecast for this market as seen through the eyes of the majority of business experts, the American government, the United Nations, and the World Health Organization.

- consumer demand sky rocketing out of control
- supply continuing to lag behind
- consumer numbers increasing rapidly
- healthy growth of consumer income
- world governments unable to cope
- an indefinite life expectancy for this market
- help needed from businesses of all sizes especially entrepreneurs

(Please see chapter two for further details.)

Our second global market is not as large as the first but its potential for yielding untapped wealth is nonetheless impressive. In the case of this global market, sub-segmentation may not be applicable but the potential for business opportunities is limitless. Experts predict that the sky could be the limit for anyone serious about wanting to take advantage of ballooning demands, minimal competitors, and massive consumer growth. As a matter of fact, the American government is begging for businesses to help narrow the ever widening gap between supply and a demand that is threatening to run away and create a worldwide problem of epic proportion.

Other world governments are also quite concerned and some are even comparing consumer demand in this market to a run-away freight train. Demand is simply outstripping supply because many businesses either do not understand consumers and their demands or they do not have the necessary expertise to develop the appropriate businesses and consequently they are failing miserably in this particular market. The United States simply has no choice but to try and meet these demands, and they are acknowledging that they need help from private industry, entrepreneurs, and businesses of all sizes. Moreover, they are willing to pay handsomely for anyone who can develop the expertise needed and supply the goods that are being demanded. Since this market is driven by demands from consumers unable to control their inherent needs, consumer growth and demand is expected to race along the track indefinitely.

Remember that many of your potential competitors are simply not taking the time to understand the WWWH concept

In 2003 18.2 million American consumers were classified as being part of this global market that was made up of about 171 million consumers. According to the experts it is estimated that this worldwide figure will be about 228 million by 2025. This means estimated annual consumer growth of well over 2 million. In addition, the World Health Organization is projecting large annual consumer growth in both India and China with an estimate of about two million consumers annually from China.

Here is the 20 year forecast for this market as seen through the eyes of the majority of business experts, the American government, the United Nations, and the World Health Organization.

- consumer demand threatening to get way out of control
- supply having difficulty keeping up
- consumer growth ballooning
- world governments having difficulty dealing with consumer demand and consumer growth
- the life expectancy for this market is indefinite
- help needed from businesses of all sizes especially entrepreneurs

(Please see chapter three for further details.)

Our third global market is somewhat different to our first two global markets in that demand is not only driven by its consumers. It is also being driven by technological factors. In addition, whereas the first two markets are made up of too few competitors, this market is filled with an overwhelming number of businesses of all sizes that are competing fast and hard for consumer attention. Be not afraid because we have some very startling news to share with you.

Believe it or not, this market is very lucrative and contains large pockets of untapped wealth despite the overflow of competitors. There are many niche segments in this market, and if you have a flare for creativity and sales, this market may be for you. The way for you to get the edge over your competitors is for you to use the WWWH concept. This market is going to be around for as long as technology continues to evolve and the Internet continues to forge ahead as one of the major ways of commerce. The beauty about this market is that consumer growth is expected to hum along for an indefinite time and consequently demand will follow along. Anyone can be a consumer in this market as long as they have access to the right type of technology.

According to some of the leading business magazines,

business experts, and leading consumer magazines, this market is flooded with companies of all shapes and sizes that are trying to customize consumer demand in order to make their business plans and strategies work. They are desperately trying to influence consumers to demand what they are offering and many companies are attempting to shape consumer demand by dictating the types of products and services that they should be buying and selling. In short, the majority of your potential competitors in this market are presently guilty of trying to control consumer behavior. In most instances this is not working. In fact this strategy is backfiring for thousands of your potential competitors and now you can have a marvelous opportunity to cash in on this picture and speed ahead of your potential competitors.

This market is still relatively new and is growing by leaps and bounds. There are several niche segments for you to discover, large pockets of untapped wealth, very lucrative opportunities, and hidden groups of consumers with specific demands. It is now up to you to use these facts to carve your advantage over your potential competitors.

In 2000 it was estimated that there were 400 million global consumers in this market, and 135 million of them were Americans. By March 2005 the number of American consumers had passed the 200 million mark and the global figure had climbed to over 888 million. This is consumer growth beyond all expectations. There is nothing standing in the way of this market's potential to offer untapped wealth. The most recent information comes from data published by Nielsen//NetRatings, ITU, and other trustworthy research.

Here is the 20 year forecast for this market as seen through the eyes of the majority of business experts, the American government, and major research companies.

- consumer demand speeding into the unknown
- supply struggling to keep up
- consumer growth increasing by leaps and bounds

- world governments struggling to meet consumer demand and consumer growth
- the life expectancy for this market is indefinite
- help needed from businesses of all sizes especially entrepreneurs

(Please see chapter four for further details.)

We turn now to our fourth and final global market that in it self possesses many interesting facets. We like to refer to this market as the one that contains hundreds of niche segments and thousands of opportunities for those who are willing to work with niche markets. Many experts are of the opinion that this market's potential is grossly under estimated because many businesses have not taken the time to fully explore the potential for untapped wealth in this untapped market. The strategy that we successfully continue to promote is the "common sense" approach whereby one uses the WWWH concept to develop services for consumers.

This market contains various groups of consumers and this is why it is made up of distinct segments. Some of the consumer groups include governments, large corporations, international companies and organizations, and individuals. In many cases, consumer demand is driven by necessity rather than by choice in this global market that knows no borders. In many countries, particularly the United States and Canada, consumers are compelled by law to seek certain services. There are also millions of consumers in countries such as those in Latin America, Europe, and Asia who drive consumer demand for this large global market.

Have no fear! This global market with all of its very lucrative and untapped segments is going to be around for an indefinite length of time. In 2003 it was estimated that 31 million of these consumers were Americans.

Here is the 20 year forecast for this market as seen through the eyes of the majority of business experts, the American government, and major research companies.

- consumer demand expected to grow healthily

- supply uncertain
- consumer growth increasing at a quick pace
- world governments looking for ways to meet consumer demand and consumer growth
- the life expectancy for this market is indefinite
- help needed from businesses of all sizes

(Please see chapter five for further details.)

We would like to conclude this chapter by giving you a few key guidelines that you can use to help you beat your competition and discover markets that are lucrative, untapped, undiscovered, niche, and hidden. Above all, we want to leave you with some strategies that can help you to discover markets that are safe for investment. We are not going to lead you into a sense of false security that these markets are safe from any loss of investment. Rather, these markets are common sense markets that can offer you untapped wealth if you only take the time to think before you leap and use the WWWH strategy. We want to show you how these markets can bring you untapped wealth rather than going with those hundreds of fool hardy get-rich schemes where over 90% of the time you end up losing the shirt off your back.

Before you decide to enter any market, be it as an investor or as a business, you need to understand the WWWH concept.

(Who is your consumer, what is your consumer demanding, why is your consumer making these demands, and how can you fulfill these demands) If you can answer these questions before you do anything else, then you have already gotten a leg up on your competition. The next thing to do is analyze the following:

Is demand greater than supply in the market that you are presently looking at? If the answer is yes then you know that this is a potential market for untapped wealth. If the answer is no then you should dig a bit deeper to see if this market is made up of distinct segments. More than likely it probably is, if it is global, and here is where you start to use these markets to determine whether or not you can create niche services or products. Remember now, don't try to look at the big picture all at once. Break down the market into segments if you can, and then start looking for niches. If you can do this then you are definitely going to be ahead of your competition, since over 90% of businesses tend to focus on the overall picture instead of first breaking it down into logical pieces. Think of it as a Math fraction that needs to be factored.

Is consumer growth expected to be on the rise for at least the next five years? If the answer is yes, this is a good sign. If no, don't even think about this market. You need to ensure that consumer growth will be healthy for at least five years as consumer growth is one of the prime factors for driving demand upwards. Is demand expected to be on the climb for at least the next five years? If yes then this too is a good sign but if no then you need to move on. You also need to see what the experts are saying about the life expectancy of the market. If the life expectancy is anything less than five years then we suggest that you think long and hard before entering this market.

In brief, you need to examine consumer growth, consumer demand, and life expectancy of the market. Any market where supply is low and demand is high is an untapped market; one that can be classified as undiscovered, hidden, and lucrative. What constitutes a niche market? A market that is made up of distinct segments where it is possible to offer specific services and products to each segment is niche.

Don't fall into the trap that so many of your potential competitors seem helpless to avoid. Avoid trying to customize consumer demand to suit your skills and resources. Do it the other way around by listening first to the pulse of the market; gathering your resources; and then attacking with full force. We have now outlined four large global markets that are relatively untapped, where wealth is yours for the taking.

CHAPTER SUMMARY

In this first chapter we have discussed how you can tap into untapped wealth through the discovery of untapped markets. We have described the meaning of untapped markets, also referred to as undiscovered or hidden markets. We have shown you how to discover these types of markets by carrying out analyses of supply, demand, consumer growth, consumer income, and life expectancy of a market. We have also shown how a market can be lucrative despite the fact that consumer income may not be as healthy as we would like it to be, because consumer demand is such that no one can afford to ignore it and world governments, especially the United States, are willing to pay big bucks for suppliers and expertise. We have introduced you to niche markets and have told you that typically niche markets can be found in markets where there are distinct segments and even sub segments and we have described a sub segment as a small section of a segment.

We have told you that in order to get a head start on your potential competitors you need to fully understand the **WWWH** concept before you do anything else. **WWWH** stands for who are your consumers, what are they demanding, why they are demanding it, and how can you fulfill these demands. If you can avoid the fatal trap that over 90% of businesses are constantly falling into then you will have half the battle won. Listen to the pulse of your intended market rather than trying to customize consumer demand to suit your skills and the services and products you want to offer.

Finally, we have introduced you to four very large global markets that are ripe for the taking.

The first global market is probably one of the largest at present, contains two distinct segments, has several sub segments, and many consumers belong to both segments. Supply is low, demand is very high, and the market's life expectancy is indefinite. Financial influence is overwhelming and consumer income is over powering. See chapters two and three for more details.

The second global market is being driven by consumer demand that is threatening to reach epidemic proportions. Supply is way behind, life expectancy is also indefinite, and world governments are begging for help from businesses of all sizes. See chapter four for more details.

The third global market is relatively new, but consumer growth and demand are both expanding relentlessly and the indefinite life expectancy is tied to changes in technology. This market contains countless competitors but there is a real opportunity to claim untapped wealth if you follow the strategy of breaking it into manageable segments and then carving out the niche markets. (See chapter five for further details.)

The fourth and final global market is made up of hundreds of niche opportunities, with thousands of pockets of untapped wealth, and consumer demand is way ahead of supply. The life expectancy for this market is tied to the ever increasing growth of international trade. See chapter six for more details.

We have built our strategies on presenting you with global markets that are relatively safe for investors, buyers, and sellers and in no way are we going to present you with get-rich quick schemes. Our success is based on showing you how to manage your own success, safely and logically.

Turn now to part two where you will meet your first global market.

PART TWO:
THE LARGEST GLOBAL
MARKET YOU WILL EVER
FIND

Welcome to the first, huge global market that is filled with untapped wealth just waiting for you to discover.

In this part we will introduce you to probably the most influential market that you will ever find in your lifetime. This market is filled with opportunities that can bring you untapped wealth. It has not yet been fully explored and that is why there are very large pockets of undiscovered wealth.

CHAPTER TWO
MARKETS WITH LIMITLESS CONSUMERS

Learn About This Explosive Market

So many of us are constantly asking ourselves what we can do to increase our earnings, find ways to boost our incomes, and make more money. Of course our TV screens are continuously showing us get-rich-quick commercials that promise us ways to make thousands of dollars every month, but what these commercials conveniently fail to explain to us are the tremendous risks involved if you decide to follow up on them. Yes, life itself is a risk, but there are common sense risks and there are very big risks. As we mentioned in chapter one, we are going to introduce you to four specific global markets and we can assure you that all four of these markets present investors with risks, but common sense risks, and definitely not foolhardy risks.

Our first global market is huge, consumer growth and consumer demand are extremely fluid, and there are two very distinct segments. However, the beauty about this vastly growing market is that it contains some very interesting dimensions and we feel that it would be important for you to learn about these because it would help you to understand it better as well as to give you a very crucial advantage over your competition.

This very huge global market is filled with consumers who are crying out for products, services, and information. According to many business experts this global market is probably going to be the most financially influential that you will ever see and America and other world governments are well aware of this fact. This global market is vitally important to all world governments and when it comes to demand versus supply we can tell you that supply is lagging way behind demand.

Let us first state these dimensions for you, while making note that this list is by no means complete. We are sure that when you have studied this list you will be able to add a few dimensions of your own. We have already mentioned a few of them in chapter one, but here is our list in its complete form.

- Demand is ballooning and threatening to get out of control
- Supply is lagging more and more behind demand
- Consumer growth is rapidly increasing and is expected to continue doing so for at least the next 25 years
- Consumer income is flourishing and is expected to continue on this path for at least the next 25 years
- Financial influence is evident and is expected to expand for at least the next 25 years
- World governments, especially the United States, are scrambling to keep up with demand
- America and others are willing and ready to pay well for any one or any business able to help them deal with these demands
- Consumer demand is made up of both products and services
- This market is made up of two distinct segments
- One of these segments is made up of several sub segments

- Consumers of this market can belong to either segment or to both, as well as to several sub segments

You may be wondering why we are so sure that consumer growth, consumer demand, and consumer income are all expected to continue on upward trends. You'll soon see why when you meet these consumers and learn some very important statistics and facts. Most important for you to know first is that not many markets would ever be able to offer you such healthy conditions whereby consumer demand, consumer income, and consumer growth are all pointing in the same direction at the same time. In addition, according to the majority of business experts all of these indicators are going to stay positive for a very long time and 25 years is only a very modest estimate. We will introduce you to the consumers of this market and then we will show you why these indicators are expected to stay positive for a very long time.

Who are they?

The first segment is comprised globally of senior citizens

By 2010 they are expected to make up about 60% of our North American population and own about 70% of our banking assets.

Now meet the special needs group, our second segment.

Let us give you a few stats for this group and describe who they are. These stats are for 2005 American consumers.

- 28 million hard of hearing
- 18 million special needs persons also diagnosed with depression
- 4.1 million blind and visually impaired

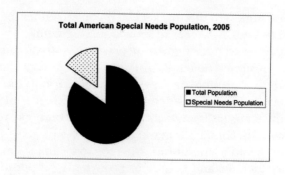

Total American Special Needs Population, 2005

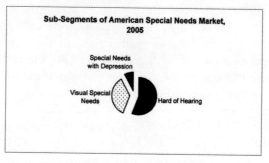

Sub-Segments of American Special Needs Market, 2005

2005 stats from the World Health Organization estimate that globally there are about 42 million blind and visually impaired persons and this figure is expected to rise to about 76 million by 2020, an increase of 55% over a period of 15 years.

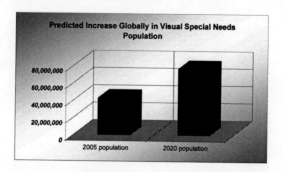

It was estimated that as of 2002 the global number of special needs persons stood at around 750 million persons and 55 million of them were Americans. This translated to one in every five Americans. In addition, as of 2002 it was also estimated that 1 in every 12 Americans were entrepreneurs and most of them were special needs persons. Finally, for that same year special needs American consumers had an estimated gross income of one trillion dollars.

As you can see from the above descriptions, the special needs segment is the one that has sub segments. As we stressed in chapter one, it is vitally important for you to break down this market into manageable pieces instead of attempting to digest the entire picture in one large gulp. So many of your potential competitors fall into the trap of trying to conceptualize the whole picture at once, and consequently they set themselves up for sure failure. If you try to look at this huge global market in this manner, you are surely going to miss discovering those very lucrative and untapped pockets of wealth. As a result you will not be able to discover those very hidden niches. On the other hand if you break this big picture down into manageable pieces, you will greatly enhance your chances of being able to tap into untapped wealth.

Each segment and every niche of this huge global market is filled with untapped wealth but your potential competitors are still not aware of this. In fact, this market as a whole is one that so many businesses of all sizes are choosing to ignore because they don't think that they can find lucrative opportunities. We are going to prove them wrong. We'll start by giving you some very potent facts before we move on to what is being demanded.

This global market will continue to live for as long as the following societal conditions continue to exist:
- aging population
- disabling diseases
- vision loss
- hearing loss

- learning and cognitive disabilities
- physical disabilities
- terrorist attacks
- war casualties

An increase in consumer growth would naturally lead to an increase in consumer demand and an increase in consumer demand would naturally put pressure on world governments to meet these demands. In turn, world governments will naturally seek the help of businesses of all sizes to help them boost and bolster supply.

What are they demanding?

We are going to provide you with a list of some of the more important demands of this huge global market. Many demands are common to both segments but there are some that may not be. We will do our best to clearly identify each demand, including those that only apply to a specific sub segment. This list, as well, is not necessarily complete. We will break this list into categories so as to make things clearer.

List of convenience services:

- delivery services from supermarkets, pharmacies, liquor stores department stores, and electronic stores (both segments)
- an increase of delivery services from restaurants and fast food outlets (both segments)
- set up and assembly services for large appliances, furniture, electronic equipment, and computers (both segments)
- pick up services from homes for large appliances, electronic equipment, and computers (both segments)
- shopping assistance at supermarkets, pharmacies, department stores, and electronic stores (both segments)

List of Internet services:

- improved access to online shopping on the Internet (both segments)
- improved hand holding customer support services from hosting companies (both segments)

- businesses to make their websites easier to access (both segments)

List of services in the travel and entertainment industry:

- an increase in services to meet the needs of both seniors and special needs persons by cruise lines and airlines
- an increase of services to meet the needs of both seniors and special needs persons by airports, railways, subways, taxi companies, and bus companies
- more tours designed for seniors and special needs persons by travel agencies
- an increase in services to meet the needs of seniors and special needs persons by restaurants, hotels, and movie complexes
- an increase of movies with captioning (the hearing impaired)
- an increase in descriptive movies (the blind and visually impaired)

List of educational services:

- easier and wider access to distance learning (both segments)
- improved technical and job training for persons with special needs
- easier and wider access to classroom courses at universities and colleges (both segments)
- improved access to adaptive technology for persons with special needs

We'll take one more moment to highlight some additional services that this very large global market is shouting for.

- easier access to banking services both by phone and on the Internet (both segments)
- more convenient ways to pay utility bills by phone and on the Internet (both segments)
- easier and wider access to accountants and financial planners who are willing to provide customized services to both segments

- easier and wider access to persons who can provide home services (both segments)

As a general observation on the part of most business experts and industry leaders, both segments are starting to increase their demands for products that are easier to use and easier to maintain. They are also pushing computer manufacturers to develop equipment that is easier for them to handle and work with and they are screaming at software companies to develop software that is easy for them to learn and use. In the case of our special needs consumers they are desperately seeking improved adaptive technology that would help them to live more fulfilling and productive lives both at home and at their offices.

We are very sure that many of you must be saying to yourselves, most of these services already exist. If you were thinking this, you are half correct. Most of these services are in place, but they are not very accessible to this huge global market and we'll tell you why in our next section. Before we move on to the next section we are going to highlight some of the more common types of products that our global market's consumers are demanding more and more of, and the types of buildings that they are presently having difficulty accessing.

Types of products:
- fitness equipment (especially for seniors and aging baby boomers)
- health and beauty products (seniors and aging baby boomers)
- products that dealing with the aging process (seniors and baby boomers)
- vitamins and herbal products (both segments)

Note: with the increasing demand for these types of products, the demands for health spas, gyms, and cosmetic services are also increasing.

According to the majority of consumers of this market some of the more common types of buildings that need to be made more accessible include:

- cinemas, movie complexes, and restaurants
- hotels, concert halls, and malls
- department stores, supermarkets, and electronics stores
- airports, subway stations, and train stations
- stadiums, sporting complexes, and gyms

We previously stated that the members of this market are also increasing their demand for information to be made more accessible to them. Allow us to list some of the more common types here before we move on to the next section.

information pertaining to investments, retirement plans, and pension plans

information on health care

- information on safety and security

Why are they demanding it?

As we have previously stated, our lists contain services and products that have been around for quite a while, but what most of these lack are the ability to take the needs of seniors and special needs persons into consideration. We are going to give you several real examples.

About 97% of all websites are not fully accessible to these people. So many websites are hard to navigate, difficult to decipher, and extremely cumbersome to deal with. Many e-commerce websites are packed with hard to understand content, tons of graphics, and complicated screens and instructions. We don't want to highlight any company in particular but we will tell you that companies like E-bay make it extremely difficult for seniors and special needs persons to buy and sell their goods and services on their websites simply because there are so many complicated menus and screens to deal with. When most of these consumers want to either buy or sell on E-bay, they need to seek assistance. Similarly, many financial institutions do not have websites that are very conducive to access by seniors and special needs persons. Many large department stores, electronic stores, and grocery chains are also guilty of presenting inaccessible websites. The majority of media websites are almost impossible for seniors and special needs persons to navigate because they are too complicated to navigate and difficult to understand. These websites are crammed tight with hundreds of links that lead you in all kinds of different directions and many of our clients compare them to mazes.

In short, inaccessible websites are driving these consumers to increase their demands.

Many consumers of this large global market are also having difficulty freely accessing buildings such as those that we have just mentioned. Too many buildings are inaccessible due to the following reasons:

- doorways and hallways are not wide enough
- doors are not well marked
- entrance and exit doors are unable to accommodate persons with wheelchairs
- many buildings lack electronic doors that are meant to accommodate both seniors and special needs persons
- there are no elevators or if there are they are not large enough to fit persons with wheelchairs
- no ramps or railings
- stairways are too narrow
- signs are difficult to read because they are either not well positioned or the print is too small
- signs are not well lit
- inadequate lighting in hallways, elevators, washrooms, and offices
- washrooms are unable to accommodate persons with wheelchairs

In short, many buildings are simply not accessible.

As for problems with the layout of buildings such as supermarkets, pharmacies, and stores, consider the following:

- shelves and displays are either too high or too low
- shelves and displays are overcrowded with merchandise making it difficult to find what one is looking for

- shelves and displays are too close to each other
- aisles are crowded with carts that are parked in the middle
- aisles are too narrow
- standing signs are often placed in the middle of entrances to supermarkets, pharmacies, and stores

In short, facility layouts are too often unable to accommodate both of our segments of consumers.

The list of difficulties goes on:

- many banks are guilty of having banking machines that are difficult for physically disabled persons to reach
- phone booths are often not large enough to accommodate wheelchairs
- clothes racks are often too heavy for seniors and special needs persons to maneuver
- airports fail to provide adequate facilities for seniors and special needs persons

The ballooning demands for businesses of all sizes to provide convenience services come about as a result too many of them not paying enough attention to what these consumers need. They are simply not listening to the pulse of this market choosing instead to offer services that are quick and dirty. So many businesses are guilty of actually refusing to provide additional convenience services because they feel that it is a waste of time to offer these types of services. They fear they would be losing revenues if they spent time offering these instead of selling their products and services. According to many business experts, too many businesses are making a huge mistake in choosing to go this route and this is why they are finding it difficult to discover the untapped wealth that could be theirs for the taking. As this huge global market continues to experience seismic consumer growth the demand for convenience services is only going to multiply and the successful businesses will be those that are willing and ready to pay attention and change their school of thought.

Both seniors and special needs persons are doubling and

tripling their efforts to find those skilled professionals who are willing to take the time to help them make safe investments, manage their financial portfolios, and help them with their annual income taxes. At the present time, many of these skilled professionals are too busy trying to gain the attention of others, and truth be told, they are not keen to leave the comfort of their offices to visit clients at home. The majority of our consumers are seeking convenient ways to deal with these financial matters and they are more than willing to pay for anyone who will go the extra mile to provide convenience. Again, many business experts are telling skilled professionals that if they choose to ignore the intensifying demands of these consumers they will be depriving themselves of a glorious opportunity to tap into untapped wealth.

In a nutshell, the majority of seniors, aging baby boomers, and special needs persons are desperately seeking the services of skilled professionals who are willing to take the time to help them keep their hard earned incomes and savings safe.

Home contractors and skilled laborers are also guilty of ignoring the demands of these very influential consumers, choosing instead to focus their sights on other types of consumers. They do not want to take the time to offer their services to seniors and special needs persons who are seeking these types of services because they are unable to do them for themselves. As time goes on, these types of demands are only going to increase as more and more persons join the ranks of seniors in particular, and home contractors and skilled laborers will be wise to start rethinking their strategies if they hope to stay competitive. These are the consumers who are going to keep you in business for a very long time. They will provide your bread and butter, plus a whole lot more, for a lifetime. They hold the key to discovering the enormous reservoir of untapped wealth and the time is ripe for you to take advantage of these market conditions and get ahead of your competition.

In short, the demand for home contractors and skilled

laborers who are willing and ready to offer services to seniors and special needs persons is rising steeply and will continue its steep ward climb for a very long time to come.

To recap, the demands that we have listed in the previous section are being driven to a large extent by:

- inaccessible websites
- poor access to many buildings
- inadequate layout of facilities
- too many businesses that do not provide adequate convenience services
- an acute lack of skilled professionals who do not understand the demands of these two segments
- home contractors and skilled laborers who are not in tune with the demands of this market

America and her sister world governments are all driving these demands because they are aware of the quickening consumer growth and consumer demand. They know that within just a few short years these consumers are going to be the majority with the most money to spend. America has already openly acknowledged this because in 1998 they passed Section 508 legislation that in part penalizes those companies who fail to make their information, services, and physical locations accessible to all if they wish to do business with the American government. Other world governments are following in America's footsteps and organizations such as the World Health Organization and the United Nations have joined the call for businesses of all sizes to heed the warnings of catastrophe if these demands are not dealt with quickly. Both businesses and individuals have an excellent chance to discover untapped wealth. This undiscovered wealth is right under your nose and all you have to do is the following:

- **R**ead about the demands of this market
- **U**nderstand their meaning
- **L**earn how to deal with them
- **E**xecute the plan

We call this strategy the "**RULE**" strategy, and it works!

How to fulfill it

There are marvelous possibilities of boundless opportunities for businesses of all sizes. The important thing to remember is that there are several potent and fluid niches that can offer you untapped wealth. In order to take advantage of this market you need to look at manageable pieces instead of trying to swallow the entire picture in one fell swoop. The demands for this market are so great and so diverse that you don't need to focus on everything all at once. Instead, turn your attention to a specific niche. One of the main keys to success in this market is for you to choose the appropriate product and/or service that are in demand. Look for a product and/or service where demand is greater than supply and competition is not as dense or hectic. This strategy would apply best for small businesses and entrepreneurs. If you already have an existing business, choose a product and/or service that will enhance your business image and/or your business offerings.

There is one very important fact we are going to make you aware of that will indeed enable you to demolish your competition. Trust us when we say that over 90% of your potential competitors are not even thinking in this way. We call it "the Ziplock" strategy and when we explain it to you it will become clearer why we named it this way.

THE ZIPLOCK STRATEGY

When we think of a Ziplock bag, we think of a bag that can be used in so many different ways. We can use it to store meat in our freezers, carry markers to school, put our cosmetics in it to take to the beach, store a wet face towel or wet bathing suit, or fill it with trail mix or cookies. The possibilities are endless. The "Ziplock" principle can also be applied to the following types of demands that we previously discussed:

- convenience services
- more accessible websites
- more accessible buildings
- better laid out facilities

These types of demands would not only benefit our seniors and special needs persons, but everyone in general. Let us look at this in a bit more detail.

More convenient services would also benefit the busy housewife, the worn-out mother with babies and toddlers, working parents, the young professional on the go, and the single person with no time to tend to their household chores.

More accessible websites would benefit cell phone users, persons using older technology, persons whose first language is not English, persons who do not use the Internet on an ongoing basis.

More accessible buildings would benefit families with lots of parcels to carry, mothers with strollers, workers going in and out with large appliances and heavy boxes and packages.

Better laid out facilities would benefit almost everyone else in addition to our seniors and special needs consumers.

If you are interested in investing in a business, setting up a business, or pursuing a career that would enable you to discover untapped wealth in this market, please turn to chapters six and seven. There you will find vital information on how to go about doing these things.

SELF EVALUATION

We are going to wrap up this chapter by presenting you with a self-evaluation. This evaluation is vitally important as a first step to finding out some important facts that will help you to analyze yourself. It will also help you to determine whether or not you are ready to seek your success in this particular market. Remember, you can take this self-test as often as you like. This evaluation was developed by us and some of our successful clients along with other business consultants and it has helped many of our clients to get a clearer picture of where they are and whether or not they are ready and able to enter this particular market.

Based on the information presented in this chapter please answer the following questions as honestly as you can. The more honest you are with yourself the better the chance for you to make the right decision.

Would you like to seek a part-time or fulltime opportunity in this market?

What type of venture would you like to pursue? (Invest in a business, set up a business, or pursue a career)

Take an inventory of the skills that you feel you may need and if you don't think you presently have them then what would you need in order to acquire them?

If you don't have all of the skills, what would it cost you to acquire them?

Would you have the time to acquire what you need?

If you either can't afford it or you don't think that you have the time then we suggest that you stop here and return to this evaluation in about six months.

Have you ever invested in a business prior to now?

Have you ever previously set up a business?

Have you had any previous experience in working with seniors?

Have you had any previous experience in working with special needs persons?

Would you prefer to work with others or on your own?

Do you like working to help others?

Are you comfortable working with computers?

Are you comfortable working with the Internet?

Would you prefer to work in a non-computer environment?

Would you prefer to work in a non-Internet environment?

CHAPTER SUMMARY

In this chapter we introduced you to our first global market that is huge and abounds with limitless opportunities and possibilities for untapped wealth to be discovered. This market is probably one of the most financially influential that you will ever find and experts are saying that its consumer growth and consumer demands are practically bottomless. For the most part businesses of all sizes are presently choosing to ignore its consumers but America and her sister world governments are desperately seeking the help of businesses of all sizes to help fulfill demands.

Demand is way ahead of supply, consumer growth is climbing steeply, disposable income is spiraling, and this market is expected to be around for a lifetime.

This huge global market contains two distinct segments, and one of those segments contains several sub segments. Consumers in this market can belong to either both segments or to several sub segments at the same time. One of the most common pitfalls that most businesses seem to be falling into these days is that they try to analyze this market from the point of view of the entire picture rather than breaking it down into more manageable pieces. There are enough niches with large pockets of untapped and undiscovered wealth so that you don't need to look elsewhere. The time is ripe for you to make your move before your potential competitors start to get wind of it.

PART THREE
EXPLODING GLOBAL
MARKETS WITH
SKYROCKETING DEMANDS
AND LIMITED SUPPLY

In part three we are going to introduce you to three distinct global markets that in their own way have abundantly rich potential and are enormously wealthy. If you learn how to analyze their consumers and the demands of those consumers, you will surely be able to tap into untapped wealth. In addition, you will learn how to dissect and decipher every segment and corner of these markets and you will be able to use our concepts to discover other similar markets on your own.

CHAPTER THREE
THE GLOBAL MARKET
WITH UNPRECEDENTED
POTENTIAL

WHY GOVERNMENTS ARE
HAVING DIFFICULTY COPING
WITH CONSUMER DEMAND

We have previously mentioned that this global market is laden with unprecedented potential due to the fact that many businesses are either simply not aware of its true existence or they do not possess the knowledge and technical know-how that would enable them to tap into its untapped wealth. At the present time many world governments including the United States are having great difficulty keeping up with this particular market's consumer demands and if they are unable to find additional resources to help them stem the tide then we could end up with a case of run away demand. In short, if we are unable to bridge the ever widening gap between supply and demand then the world as a whole will be facing a tsunami situation sooner rather than later. With all of these facts in mind and against a background of limitless consumer growth it's time for you to know who these consumers are, but before this let us again examine some important stats.

As of 2003 this particular global market consisted of about 171 million consumers and 18.2 million of them were Americans. The experts are predicting that by 2025 the number of these consumers worldwide could reach 228 million, and that means that we could be witnessing a growth of well over two million annually for at least the next 20 years. According to the World Health Organization this is only a modest estimate. China is expected to contribute around two million of these consumers annually, and Hispanics in America are also expected to make large annual contributions to consumer growth. In addition, the WHO is saying that India is expected to follow this trend. It should be noted here that Hispanics make up the second largest ethnic grouping of Americans, as well as the fastest growing group. Another notable dimension of this market is that one in every three American kids is one of these unique consumers. This market we have been discussing is made up of those who are diabetics.

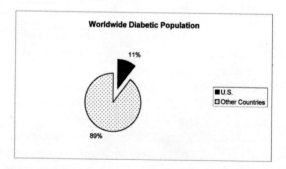

As you can see this particular market consists of consumers of all ages and its hundreds of millions of global consumers are in dire need of both products and services. The youngest consumer could be just a toddler and the oldest could be a senior.

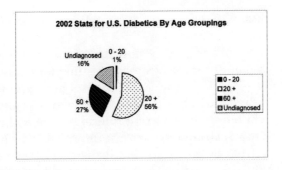

As many of you know, diabetes unmanaged can be a very disabling disease. Having type 2 diabetes, the most common form of the disease, increases your risk for many serious complications, such as include: heart disease, blindness, nerve damage, and kidney damage. The saddest part of this is that no one is immune to the clutches of diabetes and America and other world governments are only too aware of the ramifications if we don't find ways pretty soon to deal with both consumer growth and consumer demand. The World Health Organization is already preaching messages of doom and gloom to world governments telling them that if they don't get help quickly from businesses of all sizes they may not be able to meet consumer demand and this may lead to a worldwide catastrophe.

We are going to give you some examples of the more typical type of consumers that make up this market. Note: These are very typical examples but all names are fictitious.

First, meet three-month-old baby Nico who was just diagnosed with diabetes. He was born with this disease because diabetes is a hereditary disease, and both his parents are diabetic. Nico looks like a healthy, normal three-month-old baby but he is diabetic and is receiving treatment from a specialist.

Next we would like you to meet eight-year-old Kelly. Kelly and her parents just found out that she is suffering from juvenile diabetes, or type 1 diabetes. One in every three

American kids is diabetic. Kelly's life style is about to change drastically.

Now we would like you to meet Rick, who until now has ignored his parents' warnings to stop eating junk food and start eating more healthily. Rick overeats and is guilty of being a couch potato. Over the years his doctor has told him to lose weight but Rick refused to listen and is now about to pay a high price. His doctor has just informed him that he is suffering from both obesity and diabetes. He is going to have to give up his crazy eating habits and trade them in for a healthy diet.

The next person we want you to meet is a young professional named Erin who has been battling diabetes for the last few years. Upon graduating from college Erin went to work as a software engineer but she has been losing her vision for the past two years due to her diabetic condition and she is now forced to seek another type of career. Approximately 9.3 million or 8.7% of all women over the age of 20 in the United States have diabetes. About one-third of them do not know it. The prevalence of diabetes is at least 2 to 4 times higher among African American, Hispanic/Latino, American Indian, and Asian/Pacific Islander women than among white women. Because of the increasing lifespan of women and the rapid growth of minority populations, the number of women in the United States at high risk for diabetes and its complications is increasing.

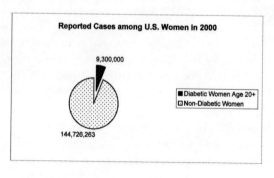

Next, meet Bruce, also a diabetic. Bruce found out about his disease about a year ago and he has decided to tackle his disease head on. He used to smoke and drink but now he is on a fitness kick. Approximately 8.7% of all men over the age of 20 in the United States have diabetes. However, almost one-third of them do not know it.

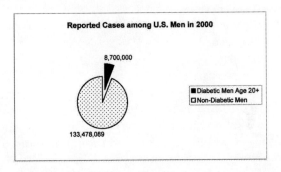

Finally we would like to introduce you to Anne. Anne is a senior who has just been advised that she will need home care in order to deal with her diabetic condition. She is not strong enough to help herself, or cook the necessary meals that she will need in order to eat a healthy diet, and she will need someone to help her get physical exercise. Approximately half of all the diabetes cases in the U.S. occur in people like Anne, who are older than 55 years of age.

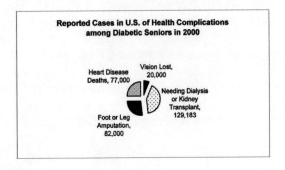

What are they demanding?

The consumers that you have just met are very typical examples of this global market. As you will learn all of their demands are very similar. First, we are going to summarize them for you. Later, we will expand on them in more detail.

The demands of this growing global market can be grouped in to specific categories as follows:

- medical services
- medical supplies
- health care
- home care
- special foods
- fitness equipment and fitness services

These are the most important demands at the present time but this list is by no means complete. We are sure that after reviewing it you would be able to add some of your own. As we stated before, these demands are common to the majority of consumers in this market. Now it's time to analyze these further.

MEDICAL SERVICES

Hundreds of millions of diabetics are increasing their demands for medical services and at the same time the American government is begging for businesses of all sizes to help them meet these types of demands. There is presently an acute shortage of both doctors and other health care professionals who possess the skills and training that focus primarily on treating persons with diabetes. Hospitals, clinics, governments, and health agencies are desperately trying to find these human resources. They are willing to pay skilled professionals very well and this is the time for you to consider this field if you are interested in working in the health care arena specializing in the treatment of diabetes. The possibilities for both satisfaction and financial stability are very real and this is a demand that is only going to grow with time.

In addition, there is desperate demand for medical

professionals to work with diabetic patients in Asia and Africa, and most particularly in China and India. These two countries are fast becoming economic powers of their own and accordingly they are ready to offer attractive salaries and personal benefits. Similarly, America is looking for health professionals to work with newly diagnosed children and young adults as juvenile diabetes, or type 1 diabetes, is becoming more and more of a concern to North America. The risk of developing this disease is higher than all other severe chronic diseases of childhood, with peak incidence occurring during puberty, around 10 to 12 years of age in girls and 12 to 14 years of age in boys.

This global market's consumers are crying out more and more for medical professionals who possess the training, skills, and knowledge to treat diabetes, professionals who will be able to handle the growing hundreds of millions of patients with diabetic symptoms and problems. Diabetes is one of the leading causes of blindness in the world at the present time and because of this many world governments especially the United States are encouraging ophthalmologists to specialize in the treatment of diabetic blindness. Similarly, the demand for nurses who can help to treat diabetics in hospitals and clinics is also spiraling.

In chapter eight we will present you with some projections for the type of income that you can expect to make if you choose to become a medical professional to these hundreds of millions of global consumers. The important thing to remember here is that these types of careers have the enormous potential to bring you immense personal satisfaction, job stability, and financial security for the rest of your lives.

MEDICAL SUPPLIES

There is absolutely no doubt that these millions of consumers are hungrily demanding medical supplies to help them combat their disabling disease and to this end America and her sister world governments are all furiously working overtime to find a reservoir of supplies that they can depend

upon on a 24/7 basis. A few companies have started to take
note of this type of demand by making medical supplies
available through the Internet but these consumers need to
have their medical supplies available through other channels,
as well. Availability through the Internet is not going to be
nearly enough if these hundreds of millions of diabetics are
to be satisfactorily served. Convenience and quickness of
service is also very important here.

Some of the more greatly demanded types of medical
supplies that are presently being sought include:
- diabetic kits
- medications for diabetics
- vitamins
- other related supplies

This list is by no means complete and we are sure that
you can add to it. This type of demand is extremely fluid
at the moment and is only going to continue in this mode
for the foreseeable future. There is a huge gaping hole that
needs to be filled by businesses of all sizes as the world as a
whole tries to wrestle with the growing seismic demand for
diabetic supplies. Now is your chance to cement your future
by either investing in a business that sells these supplies or by
opening your own business. The opportunities are definitely
not limited to America but in order to ensure your financial
security you need to obtain the appropriate skills and
knowledge. World governments are more than willing to pay
well for these supplies and you can be assured that if you can
either set up your own business to sell these supplies or invest
in a company that already sells these supplies you will be
making an important step towards securing personal wealth.
In chapter seven we will show you what types of businesses
you can either invest in or establish in order to meet these
demands.

HEALTH CARE

The health experts are warning all world governments
that health care services need to be drastically increased

in order to meet the demand of our global diabetics. The World Health Organization is predicting that if these health care services are not provided soon a tsunami-like epidemic will start to make its presence felt. World governments are aware of these dire warnings but they can't fix the problems by themselves and this is why they are strongly encouraging agencies and businesses to step up to the plate. They are ready to offer all types of financial incentives and bonuses to both individuals and businesses alike because they absolutely do not have any choice in the matter. They have to meet demands no matter what and in this instance you can help yourself to secure your own financial future and personal satisfaction by becoming a part either of the health professionals or health establishments that are needed so badly. Rest assured that you would be investing your time, efforts, and financial investments in an extremely safe area.

HOME CARE

Many diabetic consumers globally are crying out for home care services and once again, world governments are offering strong incentives to both individuals and businesses of all sizes. World governments are under enormous pressure to meet these demands because many diabetics are unable to adequately care for themselves at home and they need special professional care to help them deal with their medical conditions.

As an individual you should give serious consideration to the field of home care as this profession has the potential to ensure your financial future and if you are thinking of setting up a home care business then now is the time. Demand is rising, supply of this type of service is very meager, and as with health care all world governments are willing and ready to compensate anyone with very attractive financial benefits as long as they possess the skills and knowledge. Please see chapter eight for more details on what type of professions the business experts are advocating as both personally satisfying and financially rewarding.

SPECIAL FOODS

This global market is made up of consumers who require special foods in order to stay healthy and remain in control of their diabetes. Along with the desperate need for these types of foods, professionals are needed to prepare these foods and make them both readily and conveniently available. These hundreds of millions of consumers have no choice and this is why they are continuing to push their demands beyond the limits.

Our world governments know this only too well and as with the other types of demands they are pushing hard for partnerships with both individuals and businesses alike to help out in this crunch. They are desperately seeking ways to make these special foods more readily available to these consumers and to develop the skills of those professionals who will be able to prepare these specialty foods as well as assist diabetics to follow the appropriate diets. Please see chapters seven and eight for further details on how you can build both successful businesses and financially successful careers.

We also want to note here that the demand for special foods is getting a great push from other types of consumers who are becoming more and more health and food conscious as they seek to live healthier lives and they are taking pages out of the diabetics' book on healthy living.

FITNESS EQUIPMENT AND FITNESS SERVICES

The demand for fitness equipment and fitness services is booming at present and the experts are saying that it will continue to grow at a very fast rate. This type of demand is not only being pushed along by our hundreds of millions of diabetics but it is also fueled by other types of consumers who are becoming more and more health conscious, in a situation similar to the demand for special foods.

There is a dire shortage of fitness professionals to handle the fitness needs of our millions of diabetics and other consumers. Health care and fitness facilities and governments are willing to compensate handsomely for persons with these types of skills. In addition, there is a widening gap between the demand for fitness supplies and their availability and many businesses are still not aware of this. These consumers are crying out for fitness supplies to be made more readily available and conveniently available.

You can learn more about how to choose the safest business, the safest investment, and the safest career in chapters seven and eight. Your competition is still not fully aware of the enormous potential for untapped wealth in this very untapped market and now is your chance to get this big head start.

Why are they demanding it?

We want to impress upon you that this demand is very real. It is not weak by any means, nor is it a fad. The list of demands that we have described are what we call demands of necessity and they are not going to go away. They will keep on increasing and if world governments are not careful they run the risk of seeing a true epidemic of run-away demand. There is absolutely no other way to face these demands but to deal with them and fulfill them.

How to fulfill these demands

When it comes to fulfilling these demands there are several alternatives for you to choose from. The future is very bright for anyone who wants to secure their financial success as well as their personal satisfaction. The important thing to remember here is that you have the potential to tap into an untapped market that is global, growing very rapidly in both consumer demand and consumer size, and life expectancy for this market is indefinite. In addition, your potential competition is light at the present time and supply is still lagging very much behind demand.

Do not fall into the trap of trying to build a business or career that would serve all global consumers. First you need to absorb the entire picture and then you should break this market down into distinct segments or niches. The niches are very easy to find and we'll show you how.

You can break this market down into segments or niches

based on the type of demand. So the niches you need to examine are:

- medical services
- medical supplies
- health care
- home care
- special foods
- fitness equipment and fitness services

As you see, there are six distinct segments or niches to become involved with. Further to this, you can also decide if you want to consider breaking down this market by country, such as consumers in the United States, North America, China and/or India, or even Latin America. We mentioned China and India because they are currently experiencing the largest growth of diabetics and the World Health Organization is telling us that this trend is expected to continue for the foreseeable future. We mentioned North America and Latin America because of their close geographic locations.

After breaking down this huge market, your next task is to decide how you want to go about working in this market and here there are three distinct alternatives for you to consider.

- set up a business
- invest in an existing business
- pursue a career

Before you make this all-important decision however, we would strongly advise that you examine every aspect of this huge untapped market with its untapped wealth. Do your research and acquire your knowledge before taking the plunge. This market is going to be around for a very long time and it is one of the safest markets that you can ever expect to find. In chapters seven and eight we will give you some pointers to help you choose the right type of business and the right type of career and we will give you an indication as to what you can expect to earn both as a business and as a professional. We have compiled these listings based on present statistics from the American government, other world governments, and other large research organizations.

SELF EVALUATION

Here again is a self-evaluation. Remember, you can take this self-test as often as you like. Based on the information presented in this chapter please answer the following questions as honestly as you can. The more honest you are with yourself the better the chance for you to make the right decision.

Would you like to seek a part-time or fulltime opportunity in this market?

What type of venture would you like to pursue? (Invest in a business, set up a business, or pursue a career)

Take an inventory of the skills that you feel you may need and if you don't think you presently have them then what would you need in order to acquire them?

If you don't have all of them, what would it cost you to acquire them?

Would you have the time to acquire what you need?

If you either can't afford it or you don't think that you have the time then we suggest that you stop here and return to this evaluation in about six months.

Have you ever invested in a business prior to now?

Have you ever previously set up a business?

Have you ever worked as a sales person?

Have you ever worked in a marketing position?

Are you a diabetic?

Do you know anyone who is a diabetic?

How much do you know about diabetes? (A little, quite a bit, quite a lot)

Do you like keeping up on important health issues?

Are you Internet savvy?

Do you like working on the Internet?

Are you comfortable dealing with clients on the Internet?

Are you comfortable dealing with clients on the phone?

Are you comfortable dealing with clients face-to-face?

Do you like learning new things on a constant basis?
Do you like multi tasking?
Do you like change?
Are you a creative thinker?
Are you a motivator?

CHAPTER SUMMARY

We have introduced you to our second global market. In 2003 this market consisted of 171 million global consumers 18.2 million of which were Americans (a little over 10%). The experts are predicting that this global market will grow to about 228 million consumers by 2025 (an annual growth of well over 2 million) with China and India expected to lead the annual growth. We also said that one in every three American kids is a consumer and we will add here that presently time there are over two million Canadian kids in this market.

We introduced you to some typical examples of the type of consumer that you would find in this market, we described the types of demands that these millions of consumers have that need to be met, we told you that these demands are very real and tangent, and we showed you how you can use these demands to tap into untapped wealth in untapped markets.

In chapters seven and eight we are going to show you the types of businesses and careers that many business experts are saying can bring you wealth for the rest of your life Whether you choose to invest in any of these businesses or set up any of these businesses yourself, or pursue any of the careers that we will be revealing to you, we can assure you without any doubt that your investment will be worth your while. These investments are safe because you will be investing in markets that will offer you unlimited consumer growth and consumer demand.

CHAPTER FOUR
THE GLOBAL MARKET WITH UNLIMITED GROWTH SUCCESS IS YOURS FOR THE TAKING

We turn now to our third global market and, as the heading states; success is indeed yours for the taking. However, we would like to expand on this a bit.

This market is relatively new in comparison to the previous two markets that we have previously discussed and its consumer size is very much larger. However, we are going to take a somewhat different approach when it comes to talking about the types of demands for this global market. We previously mentioned that this global market is growing by leaps and bounds and its consumer demand is being driven by ever evolving technology. In 2000 the estimated number of global consumers was at around 400 million and 135 million of these were Americans. By March of 2005 it was estimated that the global figure had grown to over 888 million and the number of Americans had increased to over 200 million.

Let us briefly examine this trend before moving on.

The consumer size for this market has more than doubled in less than five years; in 2000 the number of American consumers accounted for about 34% of total global consumers;

and by March 2005 American consumers made up about 22.6% of total number of global users.

Despite this drop in the number of American consumers it should be noted here that as of March 2005 America as a country had the largest number of consumers both percentage wise and number wise out distancing its closest rival by more than 12% and over 128 million respectively.

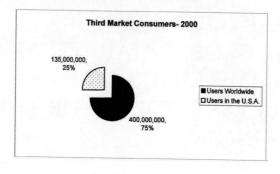

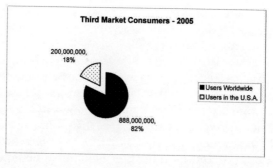

As you can see this market is in no way lacking for consumers and the forecast for this market is exceedingly healthy, with a life expectancy that is indefinite. For as long as there is technological progress and for as long as the Internet continues to be another way of doing business and of providing information, this market will continue to live with consumer demand that is being described as "unknown". There are a few important facts, however, that we would like to repeat before moving on because these facts will definitely help you to get a head start on your competition. We also want to caution you that you should not be fooled by the size of this market as most of your competition has been. It has been proving to be a very costly blunder for them.

Here they are once more.

- This global market is over crowded with business of all sizes
- The businesses are attempting to customize customer demand to suit what they are selling
- Businesses are not listening to what consumers are demanding
- Many consumers are demanding services that are in short supply
- Many businesses are only looking at the big picture instead of trying to examine the pieces that make up the big picture
- There are large pockets of untapped wealth in this market
- There are many niches or segments that are still untapped
- Anyone of any age can be considered a consumer in this global market

Because of the complexity and size of this market we are going to change the format in which we will present you with the important facts using the WWWH concept. Based on the current success of our strategies, feedback and success of our clients, and input from other business experts, as well as stats gathered from several research companies including Nielsen, Fortune 500 and the New York Times, we are going to present you with some very distinct segments or niches where we feel that you would be able to carve your success by tapping into untapped wealth. At the present time most of your potential competition is just too busy trying to force consumers to do things their way instead of taking some time to feel the pulse of the market. Consequently they are ignoring certain types of demands.

Let us first introduce you to our proposed niches and after this we will examine each one of them in more detail.

- Cell phone users
- Distance learning consumers
- The growing group of entrepreneurs
- The generation that did not grow up with computer technology
- Special needs consumers

Many of our clients continue to enjoy immense success in these corners of this vast global market and they are finding that if they stick to these corners they stand a much better chance of not being over run or wiped out by their competition.

We would like you to think of it like this:

There is a huge ice skating rink with hundreds of skaters all trying to run each other over in order to be able to skate in the center ice area. However, in each corner of the rink there are small groups of skaters who are having a great time skating around because they have been able to find a secluded area where they can skate without having to worry about being run over. Those competing for the center ice area appear to be frustrated and angry while those in the corners are having fun and they look very happy.

CELL PHONE USERS

We don't think that you would be surprised to learn that at the present time there are over 1 billion cell phone users worldwide. According to stats for 2005 this is the number that is being bandied about and further to this the research companies are saying that on a daily basis over 300 million persons use their cell phones to keep in touch. Cell phone users presently make up the majority of wireless users and their demands are growing at a very healthy rate. In addition, the number of cell phone users for 1995 (10 years ago) was greater than the entire birth rate for North America so just imagine what it would be for 2005.

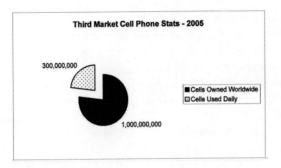

Who are they?

Cell phone users can be found in all age groups and in general they all have very specific demands. Let's look a bit closer at this fast growing global group. Yes indeed, they are global and they are everywhere to be seen. However, we would point out that the demands of cell phone users are generally very similar to those who use other types of wireless devices. Here are some typical examples of who these users could be.

- the nine-year-old youngster who uses his/her cell phone to play games on the Internet, or the teenager who uses a cell phone to surf the Internet for fun websites
- the professional who uses either a cell phone or some other type of hand held device to research some information on the Internet
- any parent who is experimenting with a hand held device to explore the Internet
- people of any country or nationality

What are they demanding?

We can tell you with confidence that all of these global users have common demands and at that too many companies are failing to meet. The experts give two basic reasons for this failure.

Many companies are still in the process of either acquiring the knowledge that would enable them to deal with these demands or they still don't quite understand the consumers' following demands.

- ability to use their cell phones to surf the Internet and download information quickly and easily
- ability to have easy fast and easy access to websites through their cell phones
- convenience of having cell phones that are easy to use, with easy to understand option menus
- cell phone software that would enable them to carry out chores and functions while away from their offices and homes
- 24/7 customer support for their cell phone service, and economic service rates

In short, these global users are demanding that companies provide them with cell phones with the ability to provide them with multi functions and convenience.

Why are they demanding these things?

As a general rule, most of us these days are seeking services and products that would enable us to do things more easily and make our lives less hectic. Our hundreds of millions of global users are no different. Cell phone users are seeking convenience and this is why they are making these types of demands. They want to have the luxury of being able to use their cell phones anywhere and at anytime to carry out tasks such as:

- downloading information from the Internet
- checking, sending and receiving emails
- checking phone messages at home and at the office
- playing games on the Internet
- paying bills

In addition to all of this, global cell phone users want to have the convenience of being able to carry out their tasks from various locations, some of which are:

- their homes and offices
- the comfort of their own backyards, or off in some remote locale
- driving in their cars
- on a plane
- on board a ship

How to fulfill these demands

We firmly believe that in order to fulfill these demands you need to be in a position to provide the necessary services and the supporting software. In addition, you will need to be able to develop those websites that are easy to navigate and easy to access. These tasks are not insurmountable if you are willing and ready to obtain the appropriate skills and knowledge. When you turn to chapters seven and eight, we will tell you the types of businesses and careers that you can either invest in, set up, and pursue in order to make yourself a true success. This segment or niche is yours for the taking. It is made up of untapped wealth, it is growing very rapidly both in consumer size and consumer demand, and life expectancy is assured for the foreseeable future.

DISTANCE LEARNING USERS

The distance learning users segment is a new addition to this huge market and at the present time their demand is starting to take off towards the skies as both world governments and institutions of higher learning seek to make it easier for students to take courses from the comfort of their homes. In addition, there are certain types of consumers who are pushing this demand upwards and the experts are saying that with time, demand for distance learning services will only get stronger. The forecast for this type of demand is very bright, but at the present time supply is scant because very few businesses have realized or discovered this corner of this huge global market.

Who are they?

We want you to meet some of the more typical types of consumers of this very interesting niche and here they are:

- adults and kids who live in remote areas and are unable to attend schools because of distance
- special needs persons who are unable to attend classes due to their disability
- seniors who are looking to take courses through the Internet because of convenience

- professionals who are too busy to attend scheduled classes because of fulltime jobs but who could learn in their homes before or after work hours
- women at home on maternity leaves or acting as caregivers for elderly parents

The National Center for Educational Statistics (NCES) notes that of the 14 million higher education students in the U.S., only 3 million students attend college full-time in residence. It noted as well that 56% of those students are women.

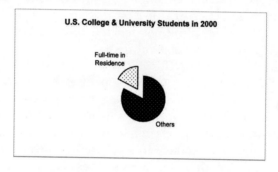

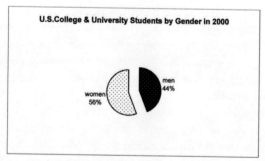

What are they demanding?

All of these consumers are increasing their demands for governments to provide funds to educational institutions so that they can offer courses through the Internet and the types of courses that are being demanded are limitless. In turn, governments are recognizing this type of demand and are more than willing to allocate funds towards the development of distance learning facilities. We are presently witnessing a growing trend among those persons who are seeking distance learning facilities to complete high school, college, and university diplomas and a marked increase in the thousands of colleges and universities offering distance learning education in order to bolster their student enrollments.

All of this results in the following:

- a rapidly growing demand for Internet courses that would enable persons to obtain high school, college, and university diplomas and degrees
- an ever-increasing demand for self-help and how-to courses
- a growing demand for distance learning courses to be made more available to more persons
- the ability for teachers, instructors, and professors to make their courses available through the Internet

Why are they demanding it?

Governments are demanding that institutions of learning develop and offer distance learning courses because it would drastically reduce the costs for building physical locations to house students; for the hiring of staff; the maintenance of schools; and other related costs.

Students are demanding the offering of more distance learning education because it reduces their costs for tuition, books, travel, and other related costs and most of all, offer them a very convenient way of learning. Educational institutions are pushing governments to spend more money on the development of distance learning facilities because this would reduce their costs and greatly increase their enrollments.

Seniors and physical-needs students are demanding more distance learning courses because it would make things a lot easier for them convenience wise. Finally, teachers are demanding that distance learning courses be encouraged so that they can find ways and opportunities to offer their own courses.

How can you fulfill these demands?

In order to be in a position to fulfill these demands you will need to do a few things. First, you need to listen to what these consumers are asking for. Next you need to find out some of the more popular types of courses that they are demanding. You then need to learn how to develop the appropriate types of websites that are vitally necessary in order to have affective distance learning facilities. You also need to do a market analysis to determine where these consumers are located.

In chapters six and seven we will give you lists of businesses and careers that you can set up, invest in, or pursue in order to help you get ahead of your competition. This niche has limitless potential and the opportunities for tapping into untapped wealth are absolutely limitless.

THE GROWING GROUP OF ENTREPRENEURS
Who are they?

As of 2002 it was estimated that 1 in every 12 Americans was an entrepreneur and since then this figure has been growing steadily. This is the group that the American government is depending on to help them bridge the gap between demand and supply in so many markets both nationally and internationally. This is the group that business experts are saying is going to carry most of the load when it comes to sparking the American economy on a continuous basis. This is the group that is presently driving a great piece of the Internet market and all the business gurus are forecasting big things for them. This is the group that so many businesses choose to deliberately ignore because they do not think that there is much financial success for them.

That last idea is so very wrong and we hope that you will take advantage of the lack of competition in this little niche to carve out your very own success. This corner of the much larger global market is growing steadily and the opportunity for finding untapped wealth is now. In addition, the entrepreneurial economies are also growing healthily in other countries and several world governments are actually encouraging the development of entrepreneurship. The business experts are saying that persons of all ages are entering the entrepreneurial arena and as more and more persons start retiring they are turning to entrepreneurship as their new career. The entrepreneurial ranks are also being buoyed by those persons who have been laid off or mad the victim of down-sizing in the past 12 to 15 years.

What are they demanding?

Many entrepreneurs are still in the process of learning how to market themselves and their services on the Internet. In addition, they are still very shaky when it comes to being able to manage their websites, their services, and their clients. According to what we are hearing these days both from our clients and fellow business watchers, some of the more critical demands coming from this group are as follows:

- a need to find hosting companies that will help them to develop meaningful websites
- a growing demand for persons to help them understand more about the rudiments of the Internet
- a demand to learn how to market themselves effectively on the Internet
- a demand for hosting companies to provide end to end support services
- a demand for educational institutions to offer courses on e commerce

Why are they demanding it?

Many of these entrepreneurs are not Internet savvy to begin with and for them the Internet is a whole new world of possibilities and opportunities. There are several things that they need to master at the same time and these include:

- learning how to work with domain names and domain registrations
- learning the importance of having websites to advertise their businesses on the Internet

- learning how to market their websites on the Internet through the use of search engines
- learning the world of e-commerce

How you can fulfill these demands

The demands and needs of this growing entrepreneurial group are somewhat different to those of companies and larger businesses and you will need to learn how to deal with customers who are not as technically savvy as bigger businesses. This niche of the market is made up of persons who are now getting their feet wet on the Internet and you will need to switch your plan of attack to more of a hand holding mode. You will also need to provide more round the clock services to them as many of them are still newcomers to the Internet and consequently more nervous whenever website connections are unexpectedly interrupted, servers go down, or their e commerce clients make unforeseen and spur of the moment requests.

Please see chapters six and seven for further details as to the types of businesses that you could invest in, set up, and careers that you can pursue, in order to enhance your chances of tapping into untapped wealth in this growing segment where competition is extremely light at the moment.

THE GENERATION THAT DID NOT GROW UP WITH COMPUTER TECHNOLOGY and SPECIAL NEEDS PERSONS

We decided to combine these last two segments because their demands are very similar and as a matter of fact they are also quite similar to our growing group of entrepreneurs. However, we want to ensure that you know exactly who they are.

Who are they?

When we think of the generation that did not grow up with computer technology two very distinct groups come to mind and here they are:

- aging baby boomers
- seniors

Just to remind you about some very important stats for this group as a whole as stated in chapters one and two:

It is estimated that by 2010 they will probably own about 70% of all banking assets in North America and they will make up about 67% of our North American population, making them one of the most financially influential groups that you may ever find.

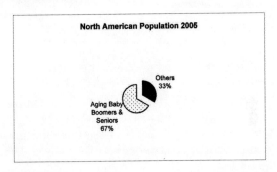

Now meet our special needs group. We are going to remind you about some of the stats stated earlier for this group, and detail who they are. These stats are for 2005 and are for our American consumers.

- The hard of hearing – 28 million.
- Special needs persons afflicted with depression – 18 million.
- The blind and visually impaired – 4.1 million.

This group spent about 4.3 billion dollars on special technology also known as access technology in 2002 and their annual net income for that year was estimated to be about one trillion dollars.

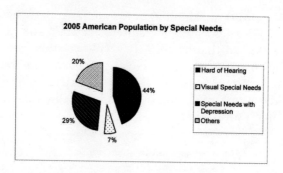

It was estimated that as of 2002 the global number of special needs persons stood at around 750 million persons and 55 million of them were Americans. This translated to one in every five Americans. The experts are saying that this segment is expected to experience consumer growth of about 10% and income growth of about 15% annually for the foreseeable future.

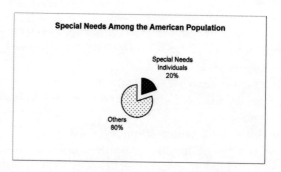

2005 stats from the World Health Organization estimate that globally there are about 42 million blind and visually impaired persons and this figure is expected to rise to about 76 million by 2020, an increase of 55% over a period of 15 years.

What are they demanding?

They have the same types of demands as the entrepreneurs but we are going to add a few more:

- greater access to computer training
- much greater access to adaptive technology also known as access technology
- the need to have websites made much more accessible
- So as to make it more convenient for you we are going to list again the demands of our entrepreneurs so that you can view all of the demands of this group on one page.
- need to find hosting companies that will help them to develop meaningful websites
- growing demand for persons to help them understand more about the rudiments of the Internet
- demand to learn how to market themselves effectively on the Internet
- demand for hosting companies to provide end to end support services
- demand for educational institutions to offer courses on e commerce

Why are they demanding it?

This segment is making these demands because of a general lack of availability of both services and products that would enable them to function adequately on the Internet. Supply is way behind demand simply because many businesses have not even given consideration to the needs of these two groups and this may be due to the following.

- Unawareness of this segment
- Lack of knowledge and skills as to how to meet these demands

There is a general feeling within the business community of North America that this segment may not be all that important but many business experts including us disagree whole heartedly. We like to refer to this fast growing group as the sleeper group that possesses lots of financial influence, offers lots of opportunities for tapping into untapped wealth and lucrative possibilities, and is a very safe segment, like all the others that we have previously described.

The American government is definitely paying attention to these consumers and is already pumping billions of dollars into this particular segment in order to meet their demands and stimulate economic activity. Other world governments are starting to take note and follow suit.

How you can fulfill these demands

In order to fulfill these demands you will need to equip yourself with the necessary skills and knowledge as to how to work with access technology, with special needs consumers, and with seniors. In addition, you will need to come up with ways to offer specialized services to this segment. Back in chapter one we said that if you had a flare for creativity and an imagination for sale then this huge global market would be for you and this is definitely true in the case of this particular segment.

In chapters seven and eight we will give you more details as to the types of businesses that you can invest in, set up, and careers that you can pursue in order to tap into this segment. If you think that your interest could lie in this particular segment then we definitely have something for you.

SELF EVALUATION

Here again is a self-evaluation. Remember, you can take this self-test as often as you like. Based on the information presented in this chapter please answer the following questions as honestly as you can. The more honest you are with yourself the better the chance for you to make the right decision.

Would you like to seek a part-time or fulltime opportunity in this market?

What type of venture would you like to pursue? (Invest in a business, set up a business, or pursue a career)

Take an inventory of the skills that you feel you may need and if you don't think you presently have them then what would you need in order to acquire them?

If you don't have all of the skills, what would it cost you to acquire them?

Would you have the time to acquire what you need?

If you either can't afford it or you don't think that you have the time then we suggest that you stop here and return to this evaluation in about six months.

Have you ever invested in a business prior to now?

Have you ever previously set up a business?

Do you like working on the Internet?

Do you like working with computers?

Do you like working with clients on the Internet?

Do you like working with clients on the phone?

Would you prefer to work in a technical position?

Are you interested in keeping up with technology?

Do you like learning new things on a continual basis?

Do you like working under pressure?

Would you like to work in a customer support position?

Do you like helping others?

Are you a patient person?

Can you multi task easily?

Are you a quick thinker?

Can you come up with quick solutions or suggestions?

Are you a good problem solver?

Do you find it easy to hold your tongue when you are being criticized?

CHAPTER SUMMARY

In this chapter we have introduced you to our third global market. A market that is still relatively new but a market that has more than doubled in a little less than five years. Americans make up most of this market's consumers both percentage wise and number wise and it has seen growth of about 48% in a little less than five years. Not shabby at all in any way.

We introduced you to specific segments of this huge market and we have suggested that these segments can hold the key to the discovery of untapped wealth. Here are the segments once again.

- cell phone users
- distance learning consumers
- the growing group of entrepreneurs
- the generation that did not grow up with computer technology
- special needs consumers

We told you that although this global market is over crowded with lots of competitors who are competing for customers, it is still very possible to tap into untapped wealth because the above mentioned niches or corners are presently being ignored and consequently there is not much competition in these niches. We described the picture of the ice skating rink filled with hundreds of skaters competing for the center ice area, whereas there are only a few skaters in the corners of the rink.

Finally we told you that at the present time many businesses are not listening to the pulse of this market but rather they are trying to customize consumer demand to suit what they are offering. The expectations for the future of this market are extremely optimistic with life expectancy being described as indefinite, consumer growth as being very healthy, and consumer demand as being extremely aggressive.

CHAPTER FIVE
THE GLOBAL MARKET THAT KNOWS NO BORDERS
THE MARKET THAT EXPERTS SAY CAN LIVE FOREVER

Welcome to our fourth and final global market.

Many business experts have coined the name "Sleeper market" for this very large global market simply because so many businesses have failed to realize its immense potential. Many of our clients, however, have been able to tap into this enormous reservoir of wealth by using our strategies and we are hoping that you too will take up the challenge and use the information here to help you race ahead of your competition and discover how to tap into untapped wealth.

For this market we advocate the "common sense" approach as you bear a few very basic characteristics in mind.

this market knows no borders

consumer demand is being driven by both necessity and choice, and is growing at a brisk rate

this market contains literally hundreds of segments

consumer growth is also intensifying at a fast clip

these consumers have money to spend

As of 2003, 31 million Spanish-Americans were members of this market. Let us give you some more numbers, worldwide, to further inform you about this market..

- 874 million of them speak Mandarin
- 366 million of them speak Hindi
- 341 million of them speak English
- 322 million of them speak Spanish
- 77 million of them speak French

Source: _Ethnologue Volume I: Languages of the World_, 14th ed. (2000).

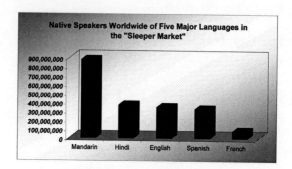

If that was the picture as of 2000, just imagine what it must be like today! As of 2003 it was estimated that about 50% of the world was made up of non-English speaking people and it is estimated that by the end of 2005 this figure would climb to about 70%. Yet for all of this English is the most spoken language in the world today. Quoting from this same source we would like to give you the following information:

English is far more world wide in its distribution than all other spoken languages. It is an official language in 52 countries as well as many small colonies and territories. In addition, 1/4 to 1/3 of the people in the world understands and speaks English to some degree. It has become the most useful language to learn for international travel and is now the de facto _language of diplomacy. In 2001, the 189 member countries in the United Nations were asked what language they wish to use for communication with embassies from other countries. More than 120 chose English, 40 selected French, and 20 wanted to use Spanish. Those who wanted English to be the common language included all of the former Soviet republics, Viet_

Nam, and most of the Arab world. English is also the dominant language in electronic communication. About 75% of the world's mail, telexes, and cables are in English. Approximately 60% of the world's radio programs are in English. About 90% of all Internet traffic is as well. However, the percentage of Internet users who are not native English speakers is increasing rapidly, especially in Asia.

Before moving on we would like to expand a bit on the difference between demand of choice and demand of necessity. Demand of choice is when consumers choose to buy a good or service. Demand of necessity is when consumers have no choice but to buy a good or service in order to either carry out trade and commerce or to help them in their daily lives. Almost every world government most of all America is forced to participate in this market and they along with many others is driving the demand for this market. It should be noted that some countries example America and Canada have legislation that dictates that in order to carry out business within their borders, businesses of all sizes must have their advertisements and other relevant materials in more than one language. Canada is a bilingual country, and America also has to satisfy the demands of their multi lingual groups such as the Spanish speaking population.

We are going to base our strategies on the following criteria:

- sources quoted above
- the United Nations findings
- what the business experts are saying
- the success of our clients in this market

For this purpose we are going to introduce you to specific niches within this market and specific services presently being demanded by these consumers. We want you to keep in mind that this global market is extremely large and is crowded with businesses of all sizes that are trying to discover their financial success but as with the global market in chapter five too many of your potential competitors are not finding it easy to carve out their success and this is mainly due to the following factors:

They are not taking the time to find those large pockets of untapped wealth

- They are too busy trying to absorb the entire picture instead of breaking it down into manageable pieces
- They are not looking in the right places
- They are thinking more about products rather than services
- They do not realize that this global market lies well beyond America and in fact has no borders
- They are not utilizing the Internet to its full capacity in order to reach their consumers

Who are they?

Your potential consumers are:

- World governments
- State governments
- Large corporations
- International businesses
- Non profit and for profit organizations
- Individuals

You are probably thinking that this list of consumers is huge and you are very right in thinking so but the trick here is to focus in on some very specific services that are being demanded; services that are at present in very short supply and are being demanded more and more because of the expansion of global trade and migration. For this reason we are going to narrow our focus to some very specific consumers and they are:

- Business professionals
- Internet based businesses
- Lawyers
- Medical professionals
- Students

We are going to deal with the demands of each group of consumers as they were listed above and based on the stats that we have presented we are going to highlight those services based on spiraling demands for services in the English language as well as those types of services that non English-speaking consumers are clamoring for. We will give you some useful pointers at the end of this chapter as to how you can attract other types of consumers. Some of our clients have and continue to experience marked success in these areas.

BUSINESS PROFESSIONALS

What are they demanding?

Many business professionals, particularly from Latin America and Asia, are seeking those persons who can provide the following types of services:

written and oral translations to and from their native language

written and oral transcriptions to and from their native language

translations and transcriptions of conferences, meetings, interviews

coaching services whereby they can learn how to carry on phone conversations and make oral presentations

writing services to help them craft emails, faxes, and letters to and from their native language

We want you to keep in mind that the term "business professionals" applies to both professionals working for businesses of all sizes and to entrepreneurs.

Why are they demanding it?

In the case of those business professionals whose first language is English, they are seeking to be able to communicate more fluently and efficiently in those languages being spoken by their consumers. Nothing can win more points for an English-speaking business professional than to have the ability to function in the language of their non-English-speaking consumers. Hundreds of thousands of American business professionals are boosting their demands for those types of services that would enable them to function more efficiently in languages such as:

- Mandarin
- Cantonese
- Japanese
- Korean
- Spanish
- French

Likewise, millions of businesses and individual entrepreneurs from Asia, Latin America, and Europe are drastically increasing their demands for persons who can help them to become more fluent and efficient in the English language, as they strive to compete in the North American markets. In addition, both English and non English business professionals alike are increasing their demands for those persons who can transcribe multiple languages because they need to keep abreast of vital statistics, market conditions, and consumer behavior in foreign markets.

We will never be able to fully emphasize how important it is for our American business professionals to have access to those types of services that give them the edge over their counterparts from Asia, Latin America, and Europe. Every single American presidency since the ending of World War II has continued to allocate more and more funds for the development of international trade. This is why these demands from our business professionals are going to keep on increasing. In short, the American government is one the main reasons for these demands and other world governments have also begun to push harder for these demands to be satisfied.

How you can fulfill these demands

Because of an ever-widening gap between demand and supply there is no time like the present for you to zero in on how you can realize some very fluid untapped wealth. You need to understand what types of services are being demanded and then you need to build your service-oriented businesses around these demands. We can tell you that there is room for both private entrepreneurs and businesses of all sizes.

You should focus on both transcription and translation types of services. With regard to transcription services you should pay attention to the following:

- transcription of electronic documents
- transcription of audiotapes
- transcription of videotapes
- transcription of DVDs and CDs
- transcription of DSS, Wav, and other similar types of files

With regard to translation services you would do well to examine the following:

- written translations of electronic documents, audio and video tapes, CDs and DVDs
- written translations of emails, faxes, letters, proposals, reports, and other types of documents
- coaching by phone, by email, and face-to-face

We want to reiterate the importance of being able to offer transcription and translation services for such things as:

- meetings
- conferences
- interviews

Many business experts are predicting that demands for these types of services will start to climb more steeply as time goes on simply because of increasing international trade activity and a growing propensity for facts to be reported more concisely and accurately during conferences, meetings, and interviews. There is, as some experts phrase it "A growing need to report facts more accurately and conveniently."

Please see chapters six and seven for more details as to the types of business investments you can make, businesses that you can set up, and careers that you can pursue in order to discover that very elusive untapped wealth.

INTERNET BASED BUSINESSES

What are they demanding?

Millions of companies around the world are crying out

for skilled translators and transcribers to help them gain the attention of those multi- lingual consumers. Internet based businesses in China need skilled translators to translate their web content from Mandarin and Cantonese to English, Spanish, French, and other languages. In fact, countless Internet based businesses in Asia as a whole are clamoring for skilled professionals to help them translate their web content. The same can be said for those numerous Internet based businesses in Latin America. In turn, millions of English speaking Internet based businesses are on the hunt for similar types of services.

These demands do not simply center on finding translators to translate web content from one language to another, but on finding business translators who can use the most appropriate business terminology of the language in question. In addition, English-speaking Internet based businesses are looking for content writers to write in language that is easy to understand, simple to read, and concise enough to remember for those hundreds of millions of consumers whose first language is not English. In a growing number of cases where more and more countries are enacting laws governing bilingualism, businesses are being legislated to publish their websites in the languages set out by their home governments. An example of this growing trend is seen in Canada where government regulations stipulate that those Canadian based businesses that are involved in doing commerce with the Canadian government must publish their websites in both English and French.

Internet based businesses are also increasing their demand for those transcribers who can transcribe DSS, Wav, and other similar types of files. More and more consumers are crying out for Internet based businesses to provide them with convenient ways to upload their files both for translation and transcription and in turn there is a mad dash to find these types of skilled translation and transcription professionals.

Internet based businesses are also being pushed by their

own multi- lingual customers who are demanding more and more that website content be published in multiple languages. For example, consumers in China are driving the demand for content on websites in China to be published in native Chinese languages first and foremost and then in English. As of March 2005, China possessed the second highest number of Internet users in the world.

As previously stated, as of 2000 it was estimated that about 90% of Internet traffic was being conducted in English but with the rapidly increasing number of non-native English-speaking consumers in Asia, the demand for translators and transcribers to provide multi-language services from Chinese to English and visa versa is spiraling at a rapid rate.

There is another factor of note that we would like to draw your attention to and this is as follows:

Many Internet based businesses particularly the large and medium sized ones are turning more and more to web developers in China and India as part of their strategy to lower their web development costs and as a result they are increasing their demands for skilled translators who will be able to act as go-betweens for the developers and the support staff for these Internet based businesses. Documents need to be translated and transcribed, as well as phone and Internet conferences. Many North American Internet based businesses are also starting to turn to web developers in Mexico as part of their efforts to reduce their internal development costs.

Why is it being demanded?

The answer to this is really not very difficult. In order to be able to compete successfully in an increasingly competitive global market, Internet based businesses really don't have a choice when it comes to attracting the attention of consumers beyond their borders, especially those who speak languages that are different to theirs. In addition, world governments are pushing harder than ever for Internet based businesses to enter into global markets as they strive to improve their own trading positions and economies of scale, as well as enhance their global images.

America is especially eager to push her Internet based businesses to engage in more global commerce and this is one of the main reasons for the demands that we have described. According to several business experts the United States is pushing even more now than ever for Internet based businesses to develop and offer multi-lingual websites that are easy to read and understand.

How you can fulfill these demands

There are definite opportunities for businesses of all sizes to take advantage of this particular niche as it will only grow in size with time. The demands are going to continue to increase and you need to think about two specific factors that will help you to reach untapped wealth long before your competition and these factors are:

- Translation
- Transcription

The opportunities to tap into untapped wealth are limitless but you need to acquire these types of skills before you do anything else. If you really want to find these huge pockets of undiscovered wealth before your competition, if you are really serious about discovering boundless financial success then you would take a close look at this very fluid niche. Do not fall into the trap that over 90% of your competitors fall into and that is:

Do not try to absorb the entire picture of this very large global market all at once.

Break it down into manageable pieces as we have suggested and examine this niche on its own.

If you would like to learn more about the types of investments that you can make, the types of businesses that you can set up, and the types of careers that you can pursue, then turn to chapters six and seven and there you will find what you will need in order to take the next important steps.

LAWYERS AND MEDICAL PROFESSIONALS

What are they demanding?

For both the lawyers and medical professionals groups

of consumers we are going to focus exclusively on North American consumers. The demands of these two groups are quite similar in nature as they are both being driven by the same types of factors. In addition, the demands themselves are also quite similar and this is why we have combined these two groups of consumers.

Both groups are steadily increasing their demands for translation and transcription services in multiple languages, especially Spanish, Cantonese, Mandarin, Japanese, French, Korean, Hindi, other populous Indian dialects, and more. They are continuously pushing their demands for:

- written translations
- written transcriptions
- audio translations
- audio transcriptions
- translations of DSS, Wav, and other types of digital files
- transcriptions of DSS, Wav, and other types of digital files
- translations of interviews, meetings, and conferences
- transcriptions of meetings, interviews, and conferences

In the case of lawyers they are greatly increasing their demands for additional multi-language services such as:

- Written translation of wills, depositions, witness statements, and court proceedings
- Audio translations of the same

In the case of medical professionals they are demanding multi-language services to cover translations and transcriptions for such things as:

- medical records and reports
- patient records and reports
- conferences, meetings, and interviews

Why is it being demanded?

According to our more successful clients, several business experts, and many World Bank officials, the following factors are mainly responsible for the demands that we have described.

- increase in international trade between North America and Asia
- increase in international trade between North America and Latin America
- steadily increasing migration of non English-speaking persons to North America
- steadily increasing migration of persons whose first language is not English to North America

It is only natural that as international trade increases at break neck speeds the demand for the services of lawyers who can prepare and execute business related documents in multiple languages will also increase. Consequently the demand for translation and transcription services will also multiply with this trend.

How you can fulfill it

Like the previous niche, there are opportunities for both entrepreneurs and businesses alike, but the trick here is to ensure that you can translate and transcribe in multiple languages. As more and more law firms and medical clinics move towards digital filing systems in order to cut down on storage costs and space, the demand for multi-language transcribers in particular is going to grow enormously. In addition, as health systems join the trend towards consolidation of patient records so that they can be more easily accessed by doctors, specialists, and other medical professionals, the need for multi-language transcription services is going to skyrocket.

It is very important for you to obtain the following skills if you want to tap into this untapped niche and discover the untapped wealth that lies here.

- translation from English to Spanish and Spanish to English
- translation from English to Cantonese and Cantonese to English

- translation from English to Mandarin and Mandarin to English
- transcription of Spanish, Mandarin, and Cantonese

We can help you to make those safe investments, set up those lucrative businesses, and find those true blue careers with the information that we will present to you in chapters six and seven.

STUDENTS

We turn now to our final niche of this very large global market. Each year North America is overwhelmed with college and university students, the majority of whom are not native English-speaking. Many of them come from Latin America and Asia and in order to function in a mainly English-speaking environment they need to obtain the services of tutors and coaches to help them to do the following:

- learn English
- understand it
- read it
- communicate efficiently in it

Most of these students come to North America in order to pursue college and university educations because they believe that the North American education system has much more to offer them than their own home education system. They come with very serious intentions and consequently they are more than prepared to pay for whatever is necessary to help them study and succeed in an English environment.

What are they demanding?

Many of these affluent students are demanding the following types of services:

- coaching services to help them with their oral communications
- coaching services to help them with their written communications
- writers to help them craft their term papers and assignments in fluent English
- translators to help them translate their thoughts and ideas from their native language to English

Why are they demanding it?

As a general rule, these students really have no choice but to find ways to exist in the North American English education system. If they can produce their assignments in flawless English then their chances of succeeding will be much better. If their assignments are not properly crafted in English, they will not have much of a chance of successfully finishing their education. It is true that many of these students who come to North America to pursue a higher education can speak enough English to get by on a daily basis but when it comes to communicating with clarity and precision, the picture is quite different. Many of these students are under enormous pressure to obtain a higher education in an English environment and the pressure is coming mainly from their parents and families, as well as the governments of their home countries.

Several governments in Asia and Latin America are very keen for their people to obtain higher education in North America. They feel that this would help to enhance their positions in the international trade arena because it would make it easier for them to do business with North America if their business professionals are able to communicate effectively and work efficiently in English. The majority of business experts wholeheartedly agree with this school of thought because they feel strongly that North Americans would prefer to do business with someone who can speak their language efficiently.

How you can fulfill it

We feel that this niche presents an abundance of opportunities for the following groups of persons to cash in and discover enormous untapped wealth in a relatively untapped market.

- entrepreneurs
- part-timers
- housewives
- those on maternity or paternity leave
- retirees

- those wanting to earn some additional income
- students

This list is by no means complete and we are sure that you will be able to add to it. The trick here is for you as an English-speaking person to have the interest and capability to teach, translate, and write.

SOME CRUCIAL POINTS

We would like to close off this chapter by sharing some pointers that several of our clients have passed on to us. These clients have found and continue to find untapped and undiscovered wealth in the niches that we have described. We hope that these pointers will help you to avoid some very typical traps and errors that many of your competitors are constantly falling into. We feel that these pointers will definitely help you to gain important advantages over your competition.

Do not try to translate or transcribe to and from too many languages at the same time. No one person can effectively translate or transcribe to and from multiple languages if they hope to offer quality service. It is impossible and those translation companies that claim to offer these types of services are only fooling themselves. What they do in order to meet their obligations is hire dozens of free lance translators and transcribers. Too often the end product is not of the best quality simply because they are trying to offer translations and transcriptions of too many languages at the same time.

Choose a handful of languages that you know that you can handle efficiently and affectively. Do not choose more than five languages. The more you narrow your focus the greater the chances for you to obtain legitimacy.

You should offer translation and transcription services as follows:

- from your mother tongue or native language to a second language
- from the second language to your mother tongue

Example: if your first language is English and your second language is Spanish, one of the most affective ways to set up your business is to offer your service as someone who can translate from Spanish to English. If you can find someone whose first language is Spanish and their second language is English then they can do the English to Spanish translations. Do not use a person whose first language is English to do a Spanish transcription.

If a person speaks English as a first language, Spanish as a second language, and French as a third language, do not use them to translate from Spanish to French or from French to Spanish. This is what so many translation companies are doing and they are constantly running into problems. Use this person to translate either from Spanish to English or from French to English, but not from English to Spanish or from English to French.

We have some dynamite suggestions for you if you would like to invest in any of the niches that we have just described, set up businesses, or pursue careers that would enable you to discover this very potent and fluid wealth. Turn to chapters six and seven for more details.

SELF EVALUATION

Here again is a self-evaluation. Remember, you can take this self-test as often as you like. Based on the information presented in this chapter please answer the following questions as honestly as you can. The more honest you are with yourself the better the chance for you to make the right decision.

Would you like to seek a part-time or fulltime opportunity in this market?

What type of venture would you like to pursue? (Invest in a business, set up a business, or pursue a career)

Take an inventory of the skills that you feel you may need and if you don't think you presently have them then what would you need in order to acquire them?

If you don't have all of the skills, what would it cost you to acquire them?

Would you have the time to acquire what you need?

If you either can't afford it or you don't think that you have the time then we suggest that you stop here and return to this evaluation in about six months.

Have you ever invested in a business prior to now?

Have you ever previously set up a business?

Are you interested in working with foreign languages?

Have you had any previous experience in working with foreign languages?

Do you speak more than one language?

Have you ever had to do any type of language translation?

Have you ever had to do any type of transcription?

Have you ever had to deal with customers on an international basis?

Have you ever traveled to a foreign country?

Are you comfortable working with other cultures other than your own?

Do you like teaching others?

Are you a patient person?

Can you deal with difficult situations easily?

Are you a good problem solver?

Are you a creative thinker?

Do you like doing research?

Are you comfortable working with clients on the Internet?

Are you comfortable dealing with clients on the phone?

CHAPTER SUMMARY

In this chapter we have told you about a very large global market that is mainly being driven by international trade and migration. This market is yours for the taking if you follow the strategy of focusing on individual niches rather than trying to digest the entire picture. Too many of your competitors fall into the trap of trying to deal with the big picture rather than breaking it down into manageable pieces. Each of the niches that we have described can offer you untapped wealth for as long as you wish. There are other niches in this market and we are sure that if you look hard enough you would be able to find them.

This market as a whole is not going to disappear for a very long time. Consumer growth is spiraling, consumer demand is skyrocketing, world governments, businesses of all sizes, and individuals are driving demand. Above all, supply is way behind demand.

Finally, we believe that your key to success lies in the ability to offer translation and transcription services. There is an acute lack of skilled translators and transcribers and the time is right for you to make your move.

PART FOUR
SUCCESSFUL BUSINESSES
AND SUCCESSFUL CAREERS

In this part we are going to give you some very potent information re the types of businesses and careers that will bring you financial stability and solid income. Knowledge of these types of businesses and careers will guarantee that you stay ahead of your competition and you will be able to reach and discover untapped wealth before they do. We can assure you that the businesses and careers that we discuss in chapters six and seven will, for the most part, be in a position to deal more than adequately with such factors as inflation, deflation, and other similar glitches in the economy.

CHAPTER SIX
BEST BUSINESSES FOR SUCCESS
HOW YOU CAN BEAT YOUR COMPETITION

In this chapter we will focus on the best businesses for success. In chapter seven we will turn our attention to the best careers for financial success. We would like to thank our many clients who have shared their ideas, suggestions, and stories with us, as well as those fellow business consultants and experts who have given of their precious time and valuable knowledge.

The trick of the trade is to be able to choose the business that has the best chance of success, but in order to do this you need to not only choose the best business but also the most suitable market. In short, you need to choose a winning combination that answers the following questions:

- Which path are you going to follow – that of an investor or of an active participant?
- Are you mentally prepared to take this all-important step?
- Are you financially ready to stay the course?

- Have you chosen what type of business you wish to either open or invest in?
- Have you done a thorough market analysis?

As we have previously stressed, the best recipe for a successful business or investment venture is one that is safe and meets the following criteria:

- You will be entering a market where demand is distinctly ahead of supply.
- Consumer growth is on an upward trend and is expected to be like this for at least the next five to 10 years.
- Consumer demand is being driven by either natural factors, or necessity, or choice, or world governments, or by consumers themselves.
- The life expectancy for the market in question is at least 10 years.
- Competition is manageable.
- The market in question contains sub segments either by type of product, type of service, or type of consumer.

We want to expound a bit on your potential competitors. In so many cases, people fail at their business ventures because they unwittingly blunder into markets that are over crowded with competitors and before you know it they have to close up shop because they are unable to offer competitive prices, products, or services. In most cases, demand may be less than supply because of the abundance of suppliers or demand may not be as strong as expected. We don't want you to be scared by all of this. Let us give you a coping strategy or two.

First, think back to that skating rink that we told you about on in chapter four. We explained to you that the majority of businesses in that particular market are busy trying to carve out their little patch of ice in the center of the rink but the corners of the rink are much less crowded and a whole lot easier to penetrate. We have shown you that it is possible to find these corners in the markets that we described, to realize your true financial success and get to that untapped wealth before your competitors you need to learn how to discover them. The key to tapping into untapped wealth is for you to discover it through market analysis. In doing your market analysis you will surely be able to minimize the competition. In short what we are telling you is that it is very possible to manage your competition.

Every now and then you hear of someone who got lucky and managed to actually create a market all on their very own by offering a unique service or product. Take, for example, the creators of the pet rock, Rubric's cube and the game Trivial Pursuit. These entrepreneur-inventors were extremely lucky and very astute, but such instances do not occur nearly as often as people might like, so we need to depend on our logic, common sense, and realistic trends. We recently learned of a young man in Canada who is well on his way to being a millionaire and we'll share his story with you before moving on.

This young fellow started off by diving for balls in the lake of a golf club. During his summer vacation while he was in high school, he used to spend his time hanging out at the golf club near to his home in Quebec and he would dive and collect the balls that were hit into the water throughout the day. At night he would take his balls home and there he would clean them and repackage them with the help of his parents and friends, then resell them to the golf club as used balls.

He took diving lessons to improve his aquatic skills and with the help of his dad, continued his little business. By the end of his high school year he was earning about $20,000 annually. He kept up his entrepreneurship during his university years and had to hire others to work with him to provide the same service to other golf clubs in his city. By the end of his final year at university, he was making about $40,000 annually and his business was really starting to flourish.

Three years after his graduation from university, this young man is well on his way. He has had to hire more employees to dive and retrieve the balls, bring them to the warehouse, clean and repackage them, and sell them back to the golf clubs. His business is growing by leaps and bounds as more and more golf clubs outside his city are seeking his services. He has even taken his business from Quebec into Ontario and is now about to sign a lucrative contract with Wal-Mart and other chains, both in Canada and the United States, that are lining up to do business with him.

When he started, this type of service was unique, but today others are trying to break in to this market because of its lucrative offerings. The thing to keep in mind here is that this young man hit upon a very unusual type of business opportunity and capitalized on it. These opportunities are once in a lifetime occurrences but they are definitely there if you take the time to really think and if you are prepared to see it through to fruition.

Based on our theories, strategies, success with our many clients, and input from them along with fellow business experts we are going to use the rest of this chapter to present you with the following;

- best businesses for entrepreneurs
- best businesses for small businesses
- best ways to expand and enhance your businesses

We will focus mainly on businesses that are most suited to the markets that we have discussed throughout this book but we will also give you some additional consumers to ponder.

We will discuss those types of businesses that the American government is desperately looking for and very willing to do business with and we will also discuss those businesses that consumers are placing more emphasis on. In many cases, the American government and consumers are both seeking the same things, but there are also opportunities to venture into businesses that can be quite successful. According to many business experts, the sky could be the limit for those persons who are willing to use their creativity and imaginations. We are also going to tell you which market would best suit the business that we suggest and we will give you some general pointers as to how to get started.

Some final important points need to be mentioned before we introduce our best businesses for success.

A consumer can belong to more than one segment or one market.

Examples: A senior who is blind, a diabetic who is a senior, a senior who is an Internet user, an Internet user who is a diabetic, and so on. Other world governments are also following the lead of America re their demands for products and services from businesses of all sizes. In general, the businesses that we present to you are not get rich quick ventures but safe and long lasting income producers. The businesses that we present to you will definitely help you to discover and tap into untapped wealth. In general, the businesses that we discuss are a lot more capable of weathering inflation and deflation storms. The businesses that we present to you can also benefit many others outside of the markets that we have presented in this book.

Here is the format that will be used for the presentation of each business:

- Type of business
- Who in particular is demanding it
- Who else can benefit (the ziploc principle)
- Which market is best suited to this type of business
- Skills required
- Some general tips to get started
- Income potential

Type of business?

HOME SERVICES BUSINESS

Who in particular is demanding this?

Seniors, aging baby boomers, special needs consumers.

Who else can benefit (the ziplock principle)?

Busy housewives, busy executives, busy mothers, and busy families.

Which market is best suited to this type of business?

See chapter two for more details on this market.

Skills required?

If you can do any of the following:

- Kitchen and bathroom repairs
- Plumbing and carpentry
- Masonry and house painting
- Masonry and home renovations

Some general tips to get started?

If you live in a small town or city, it is possible for you to offer your home services as a lone entrepreneur to start with, but if you live in a larger city, it may be more advantageous to partner with one or two others. Many seniors and special needs persons are constantly looking for handy men to help them do anything from home renovations to changing a bulb, or from changing a lock on their doors to assembling furniture. Two years ago, one of our clients started a small home service business whereby he employed three of his more able-bodied senior friends. Together they started to offer their services to senior citizens' complexes and special needs consumers. They charged reasonable prices to their clients and a minimal fee to anyone who wanted to join their band of tradesmen. Before starting they advertised to senior citizens' complexes and put up ads in doctors' offices, clinics, pharmacies, and supermarkets.

Income potential?

They started slowly at first, running the business out of our client's home, but after about a year they sought larger facilities. Two years, 10 tradesmen and over two hundred clients later, they are making a healthy six figure profit. They have even expanded their services to include tailoring and sewing services and they also offer utility services such as changing light bulbs, and fixing and changing locks.

Type of business?

HOME CARE BUSINESS.

Who in particular is demanding it?

Seniors, diabetics, health care systems, the American government, other world governments.

Who else can benefit (the ziplock principle)?

Cancer patients, heart patients, others suffering from disabling diseases.

Which market is best suited to this type of business?

See chapters two and three for further details.

Skills required?

If you have a nursing background or you are a health care professional.

Some general tips to get started?

We feel that the home care business is very suitable to an entrepreneur in that they can map out their own agenda, deciding how much work to take on, what hours to work, and where to work. The demand for home care services is increasing rapidly, so the opportunity for home care professionals to band together and venture into a small home care business is very real and the financial rewards are very impressive. We will stipulate though that both the American government and health care systems alike are looking for very skilled and dedicated home care professionals. It is possible to have your business base from home, as almost all of your services would be carried out at your client's homes, but you can certainly use your own home for all those business accounting functions. You can advertise your services at hospitals, clinics, doctors' offices, and senior citizens' complexes.

Income potential?

Several of our clients operate as entrepreneurs, and their average annual income fluctuates between $50,000 to $75,000. However, some of our fellow business experts tell us that some small home care services businesses are making upwards of about one million annually. Due to the increasing demands we expect incomes for this type of business to climb over the next few years.

Type of business?

FINANCIAL SERVICES.

Who in particular is demanding it?

Seniors, aging baby boomers.

Who else can benefit (the Ziplock principle)?

Entrepreneurs, busy professionals, accounting firms, financial institutions.

Which market is best suited to this type of business?

See chapter two.

Skills required?

- accounting
- financial planning
- insurance services

Some general tips to get started?

We know of several entrepreneurs who operate successfully out of their homes. They provide services where their clients either come to them or they go to their clients. We have found that on the whole, this type of business is a good fit for those who wish to become entrepreneurs because they have more latitude and flexibility to offer different types of services and they can work more freely with their clients. These types of consumers prefer to deal with entrepreneurs because they are often intimidated by those large accounting firms and financial planners at the banks. Many of the consumers who are seeking these types of services are most concerned about keeping their savings and investment portfolios safe. Some of our more successful entrepreneurs offer such services as:

- Income tax preparation
- Financial planning
- Portfolio investment
- Home insurance services

You can advertise your services at senior citizens' complexes, large accounting firms and insurance companies, and in malls. The trick here is to win the trust of both consumers and businesses alike.

Income potential?

Based on information that we have gathered and surveys out there we can tell you that anyone who chooses to venture into this type of business can expect to make about $25,000 on a part-time basis, but that they could potentially triple this if they were to make it a fulltime venture.

Type of business?

TRAVEL AGENCY

Who in particular is demanding it?

Seniors, special needs persons, and aging baby boomers.

Who else can benefit (the Ziplock principle)?

Families with young kids, busy professionals, and singles.

Larger travel agencies are looking for smaller travel agencies to help them provide services more efficiently and effectively. Large cruise lines and tour companies are seeking the services of smaller and more personalized travel agencies.

Which market is best suited to this type of business?

See chapter two.

Skills required?

- Are you a travel agent or a budding travel agent?
- Do you love traveling yourself?
- Do you like interacting with others?
- Do you like doing research on sunny destinations, winter getaways, ski holidays, and much more?

Some general tips to get started?

We feel that it will be easier for you to get started if you already own your own travel agency. You can expand your agency to cater to the needs of the consumers listed above by offering services such as the following:

Door to door services to include pick up from home, airport services, meeting and assisting, personalized and customized services if the client is taking a cruise or tour, and, finally, transportation back to the client's home upon return from the trip. Special cruises, bus tours, and train trips that would accommodate the needs of seniors and special needs persons. Helpful services to include providing customers with useful information on desired destinations.

You can advertise your services at large travel agencies,

senior citizens' complexes, agencies for special needs persons, and in weekend newspapers. We do have an insider secret to share with you that will show how serious the American government is about catering to the needs of both seniors and special needs persons. By mid 2005, we expect to see the American government enact legislation pushing cruise lines to make their ships and liners more accessible to consumers in particular to seniors and special needs persons. What more evidence do you need?

Income potential?

We know of a few travel agencies who, after implementing some of the services that we listed above, have been able to triple their annual incomes. We can tell you the income potential here is only going to get better as more seniors and aging baby boomers seek these types of services. The potential for a six and seven figure annual income is quite realistic.

Type of business?

STORES THAT SELL PRODUCTS FOR DIABETICS.

Who in particular is demanding it?

Diabetics, the American government, other world governments, health care systems.

Who else can benefit (the Ziplock principle)?

Those who are on special diets, those looking to live more healthily.

Which market is best suited to this type of business?

See chapter three for more details.

Skills required?

- If you have a medical background or you are a health care professional then you are way ahead of the game.
- If you like to be in the sales or marketing fields then this type of business may be for you.
- If you are a "people person", enjoy working in the health care field, and are prepared to offer round the clock customer support, you may enjoy this type of business venture.

Some general tips to get started?

Make sure you are familiar with everything you need to know about diabetes. You may also want to think of offering an online store for diabetics on the Internet. In this case you need to learn how to operate an online business in addition to the other skills that we have listed. We strongly recommend that you seek professional help before venturing into such a business. The financial outlay may be quite substantial if you do not have the appropriate Internet skills required. Make sure that you are fully knowledgeable about the ins and outs of e-commerce.

For example, you would need to know, or learn, how to set up a website, work with e-commerce customers, and provide shipping services to them. Our strong advice would be for you to investigate thoroughly before starting. If you have all of these skills then the financial rewards are yours for the taking but if you don't then you should seek trusted partners. We would like to stress that an Internet based store may be more lucrative for you if you can manage it, but there is nothing wrong either with having a regular type of store. Just make sure that it is well located, convenient to reach and accessible, that the physical layout is easy to negotiate, and that business hours are convenient. You may want to consider a six day work week with some service on a Sunday. If you set up an online store, make sure that your search engine optimization is well done so that you do not have difficulty attracting the right type of customers to your website and they do not have difficulty finding you. If you choose to set up a regular store, you can advertise in the following places:

- doctors' offices
- medical clinics
- pharmacies
- hospitals
- health clubs
- malls

Income potential?

If all of your skills are in place, the potential for financial success and discovery of untapped wealth is unlimited. Through an online store you could attract global customers including governments, individual consumers, and organizations. The potential for six and seven figure annual incomes is a definite with an Internet based business but you may have to work harder with a regular based store as you will need to spend more time advertising.

One final note about this business: The American and other governments are truly anxious to find those businesses that will be able to sell products for diabetics on a 24/7 basis.

Type of business?

FITNESS EQUIPMENT STORES

Who in particular is demanding it?

Seniors, special needs persons, diabetics, and aging baby boomers.

Who else can benefit (the Ziplock principle)?

Those who are desirous of staying fit (hundreds of millions of global consumers).

Which market is best suited to this type of business?

See chapters two and three.

Skills required?

You should have some sales and marketing skills along with a propensity to work with people.

You should also have a keen interest in the fitness field and you should be able to deal with customers who are going to continuously test your patience and propensity for problem solving.

In addition, we strongly believe that you should have the following:

- be analytical
- be market driven
- be customer driven
- be a good problem solver
- be able to think fast on your feet

- be able to come across as someone who knows their products well

Some general tips to get started?

We know of some persons who have attempted this type of business on their own. It has been difficult, simply because there are several things to manage all at the same time, so we do advise that this should be a small business venture. Make sure that you know what types of fitness equipment your consumers are looking for. This would mean that you should carry out a market analysis of your target market. We feel that a regular store may be better for you to start with because it would help you to iron out any glitches before you go the Internet route. If you choose to start with a regular type of store then you should ensure that the location of your store and your business hours are convenient, and that the layout of your store is accessible and easy for everyone to negotiate.

It may not be essential for you to have a 24/7 business, but business hours could include six days of regular hours and maybe a seventh day of a few hours.

You can advertise at any of the following locations:

- gyms
- health clubs and spas
- senior citizens complexes
- medical clinics and doctors' offices
- pharmacies
- large corporations
- supermarkets

Income potential?

We are quite confident that a business such as this can bring you a six figure annual income, but we also feel that in order to be successful you should consider a small business venture as opposed to a gargantuan effort. If you are feeling overwhelmed by all of the tasks that you need to accomplish then a regular type of store may be the best bet to start with. If you choose the Internet route for your fitness store, the potential for attracting global consumers is much better, but we remind you to ensure you are fully Internet and e-commerce savvy. In short, we feel that the Internet alternative will give you a better chance at obtaining untapped income but be careful to ensure that you are fully prepared.

Type of business?

eBay AGENT SERVICES.

Who in particular is demanding it?

Internet users, entrepreneurs, small businesses.

Who else can benefit (the Ziplock principle)?

Retirees, pre-retirees, special needs persons.

Which market is best suited to this type of business?

See chapters two, four, and five.

Skills required?

In order to be a highly functioning eBay agent you will need to know all the ins and outs of how to buy and sell effectively on eBay. In addition, you would need to sharpen your online or Internet marketing skills to the sharpest edge possible. You will need to know when to buy, when to sell, and for how much. In addition, your writing skills will need to be very good as you will be called upon at every step to write product descriptions that are tempting and hard to turn down. In short, if you like sales and marketing, this type of business is for you.

Some general tips to get started?

Learn how to function on the Internet.

Learn all you can about how to buy and sell on Ebay.

Sharpen up your writing skills.

Advertise through your own website, in malls, and at small business associations.

Income potential?

We believe that one can become a very successful EBay agent either as an entrepreneur or as a small business owner. The key to success is skill and the ability to market one's service. We presently have individual entrepreneurial clients who earn over six figure incomes as well as small business clients who are actually making seven figure annual incomes.

Type of business?
DISTANCE LEARNING DEVELOPMENT SERVICES.
Who in particular is demanding it?
Entrepreneurs, seniors, aging baby boomers, special needs persons.
Who else can benefit (the Ziploc principle)?
Students living in remote areas, world governments, universities, colleges, high schools.
Which market is best suited to this type of business?
See chapters two and four.
Skills required?
You'll need an in-depth knowledge of how to develop websites that can accommodate distance learning courses. You can either be a super website developer or one that can develop and write materials for distance learning courses. The development and writing skills here are extremely important as you will need to be able to offer courses for a new type of audience, an Internet audience. The learning process here will be much different to that of being in a classroom. You will need to have a great love and passion for the education field.

Some general tips to get started?
We believe that this type of business may be more suited to teachers and specialized website designers and developers. You can take either skill outlined here and market yourself as a distance learning consultant or as a distance learning developer. There is room for both entrepreneurs and small businesses. You can advertise yourself to colleges, universities and any other type of learning institution, government agencies that are associated or affiliated with institutions of learning, and independent chartered accounting or financial institutions that offer diploma certifications.

Income potential?
We are aware of a few independent consultants who make healthy five figure annual incomes but we would like to stress that the demand for distance learning is rapidly increasing

mainly due to several governments, especially America, who are really promoting this type of learning. The future for potential and untapped income is exceedingly bright and we really like what we are seeing for this type of business.

Type of business?

TRANSLATION SERVICES.

Who in particular is demanding it?

Immigrants coming from Latin America and Asia to North America, persons whose first language is not English, and persons from North America wishing to trade in Latin America, Asia, and Europe.

Who else can benefit (the Ziplock principle)?

Foreign students coming from countries where English is the second language,

international businesses and corporations, and website owners wishing to provide multi lingual services.

Which market is best suited to this type of business?

See chapters four and five.

Skills required?

You should either be able to speak more than one language, or have access to persons who speak more than one language. You should also have access to persons who can provide both written and audio translations. A passion for/or enjoyment of multi cultural environments would also be a great asset.

Some general tips to get started?

Most of our more successful translation services clients stay well away from providing translation services in too many languages. They do not provide translation services in more than five languages at the very most because translations in any more than five languages start to affect your company's image. Realistically, no one can adequately provide services in more than a few languages and expect to remain efficient at the same time. Too many translation companies claim that they can translate in so many languages, and in order to live up to their promise of offering these types of services, they are very often guilty of having to hire translators who are not always quite able to step up to the plate. In addition, many translation companies make the error of offering services that says that they can translate to and from second languages to third languages.

Here is a basic example: The ABC Company says that it can offer translations from English to Spanish and visa versa, English to French and visa versa, Spanish to French and visa versa. The pitfall here is to say that this company can offer services from Spanish to French and visa versa.

The best solution here is to offer translations to and from a mother tongue. In short, translators can translate to and from their mother tongue, but not to and from a second language to a third language.

Places to advertise would be:

- printing companies
- immigration services agencies, lawyers and doctors that deal with clients and patients whose first language is not English
- international organizations and agencies

We feel strongly that this type of business is best suited to the entrepreneur but there is nothing wrong in expanding later on.

Income potential?

Most of our clients who have chosen to go into the translation business have done so as entrepreneurs and in general they have been able to sustain a healthy five figure annual income. This field is growing and with time the experts are saying that the growth in international trade and migration will only improve the chances for discovering untapped wealth.

Type of business?

COACHING SERVICES IN MULTIPLE LANGUAGES.

Who in particular is demanding it?

North American business professionals wishing to do business in countries where English is the second language, and foreign business professionals wishing to do business in North America whose second language is English.

Who else can benefit (the Ziplock principle)?

Foreign students studying in North America whose second language is English.

Which market is best suited to this type of business?

See chapter five.

Skills required?

- a flare for languages
- an interest in working with people
- a propensity to be a good and patient teacher
- a basic knowledge of the culture of the second language that you wish to work with

Some general tips to get started?

You should stick to working with just two languages, your mother tongue and a second language. Provide your coaching services in your mother tongue. Example: If your mother tongue is English and your second language is Spanish, offer your services to Spanish speaking consumers to help them become proficient in the English language. Some of our more successful clients in this type of business offer coaching services to improve oral and phone conversations, as well as coaching services to improve writing skills for letters, faxes, emails, and other types of documents.

You can advertise at colleges and universities, international businesses, organizations and agencies, immigration agencies, and any other location that is involved with international commerce.

We would recommend that you start off as an entrepreneur. After you have established yourself, you may want to seek partners. We feel that it is safer to do it this way.

Income potential?

Most of our more successful clients have chosen to operate as entrepreneurs but we do know of a few successful small businesses. On average our entrepreneurial clients make a very healthy five figure annual income. This field is growing and will continue to do so as international trade and business continues to prosper and spread among world economies. In short, the future is very bright for anyone who wishes to discover untapped wealth through this type of business.

Best ways to expand and enhance your businesses

We would like to give you some vital tips about enhancing and expanding your existing businesses and how you can attract more customers, increase your revenues, and cut your costs.

SERVICES

Enhance your services to include features such as:

- delivery and pick-up
- installation
- assembly
- convenient hours of business
- round the clock hours if applicable
- phone and Internet services
- person-to-person or face-to-face services

WEBSITES

Design and develop your websites to accommodate:

- mainstream users
- seniors and aging baby boomers
- special needs persons
- cell phone users
- persons who use older and slower technology
- persons who use slower Internet connections
- persons whose first language is not English

Ensure that your buildings are well located and accessible, and that the physical layout is accessible to all. Those of our clients who have followed our suggestions for enhancing their services have seen an increase of customers of approximately 35%. Those of our clients who have chosen to follow our suggestions for improving their websites have been able to see the following results:

- reduction in internal costs of about 40%

- reduction in external costs of about 25%
- increase in customers of about 30%
- increase in revenues of about 35%

Finally, several of our clients who have taken our advice re improving the accessibility to their buildings and their displays and facilities have seen a jump of approximately 15% increase in their customer base.

CHAPTER SUMMARY

In this chapter we have given you a list of businesses that we feel can help you to discover untapped wealth and race ahead of your competition. We have described businesses that will have excellent chances to thrive in the markets that we have discussed in previous chapters and we have shown you how these businesses can attract other types of consumers. We have also told you that in addition to meeting the demands of consumers, these businesses will also meet the demands of businesses of all sizes, world governments, especially America, and international organizations and agencies. We also feel that service-oriented businesses have a much better chance of success in these markets than product-oriented businesses. There are, however, certain product-oriented businesses that can help you to find that very lucrative income.

Our lists are by no means complete but we are sure that you can use them to discover other types of lucrative opportunities. Some of our clients asked us to mention the following types of businesses as well and they wanted us to tell you that they are using them to gain part-time income and are even using them to get their youngsters started on the road to entrepreneurship.

- home cleaning service
- dry cleaning service
- catering service
- dog walking service
- pet sitting service
- outdoor maintenance service for all seasons
- personal shopping service
- beauty salon home service
- hairdressing home service

CHAPTER SEVEN
THE RIGHT CAREER FOR TRUE SUCCESS
THE AMERICAN GOVERNMENT IS WILLING TO PAY YOU BIG BUCKS

As we promised in earlier chapters, we are going to devote this chapter to giving you a list of careers that many business experts feel will help you procure a most satisfactory financial income, for as long as you wish. We honestly feel that these types of careers are very important because they are the skills and professions that many world governments, especially the United States, need so badly. They are also the skills and professions that hundreds of millions of consumers are depending on to help meet their demands. They are the skills and professions that businesses of all sizes are seeking because they need them in order to stay alive and feed their business life lines and they are also the skills and professions that will help the global economy to survive.

As we have been advocating throughout our book, we are not going to direct you to any kind of get-rich-quick schemes nor are we going to direct you to those schemes that can separate you from your hard earned money. The careers we will discuss here are careers that will definitely help you to discover untapped wealth, become highly sought after and highly paid experts, and bring you both personal and financial success.

The American government is willing to pay handsomely for these types of skills and professions. Other global governments are also willing to pay you if you can show that you have the skills, tenacity, motivation, and creativity to stay in your chosen profession or career. Most of all, millions of consumers are willing to pay for your services and expertise. We can't stress enough how important it is for all of these stakeholders to be able to have access to these types of skills and professions and if you are really serious about finding that very hidden and untapped wealth you will spare a few minutes to inspect and give your full attention to the rest of this chapter. We are confident that after learning about these types of skills and professions, you will agree that these are the common sense and logical careers to bring you safely to financial stability.

These lists are by no means complete, nor are they listed in any order of importance. However, as in chapter six, we are going to present each skill and career in a specific format so as to clarify things a bit more for you.

Before getting started we want to remind you of a few important points.

- First, the key to success in any career is for you to choose one that you can enjoy, devote your professional time to, and obtain your financial goals.
- Second, before you take that all important step of choosing your career, you should ensure that you will be able to find a market for your skills and/or profession.
- Third, you should ascertain that the market that you are aiming your skill and/or career towards will be around for at least the next 10 years.
- Fourth, you should determine if the career you choose

or the skill you obtain are those where supply is less than demand in the market you are focusing on.

- Fifth, you should be constantly monitoring the labor market to ensure that your career or skill is still in demand. We suggest that you do this every six months.
- Sixth, you should never leave home without a backup career plan in your back pocket.
- Seventh, you should always be prepared to switch careers if your present one is in jeopardy of being cut short either by layoff, down sizing, for health reasons, or circumstances beyond your control.

We are going to make use of the following format that will cover both skills and careers that most business experts, the American government, other world governments, the United Nations, the World Health Organization, several leading business magazines, and big businesses feel are those sure to be in the greatest demand for at least the next 10 years. We are also going to categorize them.

Here is the format:
- Type of career/skill?
- Who is demanding it?
- Why is it being demanded?
- Potential outcome?

Now, let us begin.

HEALTH PROFESSIONALS

Type of career/skill?

Family physicians specializing in geriatrics.

Who is demanding it?

The American government, other world governments, the World Health Organization, millions of seniors and aging baby boomers worldwide.

Why is it being demanded?

To meet the needs of an aging global population.

Potential outlook?

A career that promises longevity and great personal and

financial rewards. Opportunities are many, both within and outside of the United States.

Type of career/skill?

Medical doctors to treat disabling diseases such as diabetes, cancer, and various heart conditions

Who is demanding it?

The American government, other world governments, the United Nations, the World Health Organization, millions of global diabetics and others.

Why is it being demanded?

To fill the seismic needs of hundreds of millions of global consumers.

Potential outlook?

This career promises longevity, unheralded personal satisfaction, and financial security. You can find opportunities almost anywhere.

Type of career/skill?

Ophthalmologists specializing in the treatment of diseases that cause blindness and loss of vision.

Who is demanding it?

The American government and her sister world governments, the World Health Organization, millions of global consumers.

Why is it being demanded?

To stem the tide of the growing number of global consumers suffering from blindness and to increase blindness prevention.

Potential outlook?

A career that is yours for as long as you desire. Financial security is guaranteed. Opportunities abound both in and out of North America.

Type of career/skill?

Plastic surgeons.

Who is demanding it?

Millions of consumers wishing to foil the aging process.

Why is it being demanded?

Millions of persons worldwide would like to retain the appearance of youth for as long as possible.

Potential outlook?

This career will be sustained by a rapidly aging population and others thus the prospects for financial stability and personal satisfaction are very bright. Opportunities are everywhere around the world.

Type of career/skill?

Surgeons specializing in hip replacements, knee related problems, and other related areas.

Who is demanding it?

Hundreds of millions of global persons, America and her fellow world governments, the World Health Organization.

Why is it being demanded?

A rapidly aging population is being accompanied by the demand to take care of those who are faced with more and more incidents of broken bones plus more.

Potential outlook?

A career that could allow you to work in many different places. You can certainly write your own ticket to personal and financial success.

Type of career/skill?

Health care and home care workers.

Who is demanding it?

All world governments, the World Health Organization, health care systems worldwide, hundreds of millions of global consumers.

Why is it being demanded?

Due to the rapid increase in an aging population as well as disabling diseases.

Potential outcome?

These types of careers present lots of opportunities for flexibility, variation in the type of job to be carried out, and both personal and financial success. In addition, this career can be pursued anywhere in the world.

Type of career/skill?

Dieticians and culinary professionals.

Who is demanding it?

Diabetics, persons on special diets because of health related issues, persons into healthy eating, America and her sister world governments.

Why is it being demanded?

To keep fit and healthy, to avoid the grip of disabling diseases.

Potential outcome?

These careers have the potential to bring you very real financial success and it can only get better as time marches on. In addition, There is lots of opportunity to work anywhere in the Western world.

Type of career/skill?

Fitness instructors.

Who is demanding it?

Millions of global fitness conscious consumers, seniors, special needs persons, large businesses and corporations.

Why is it being demanded?

More and more persons are seeking to live healthily through keeping fit, diabetics and those suffering from other disabling diseases need to bring fitness into their lives in order to deal with their afflictions, large corporations and businesses are using fitness instructors to help their employees deal more effectively with stress.

Potential outcome?

Marvelous opportunities to reap financial success on an ongoing basis. Opportunities can be found both in and out of North America and in several different types of environments.

Type of career/skill?

Massage therapists, physiotherapists, and occupational therapists.

Who is demanding it?

America and other world governments, large corporations and businesses, seniors, special needs persons, millions of others.

Why is it being demanded?

To cope with various disabilities, stress related problems, physical diseases, age related problems.

Potential outcome?

These types of careers can potentially bring you ongoing income for as long as you wish. Even after you have decided to retire you will be able to live comfortably off the wealth that you have been able to amass in the pursuit of these types of careers. You could have the opportunity to work in any country that needs these types of services.

Type of career/skill?

Psychologists, psychiatrists, and psychotherapists.

Who is demanding it?

America, other world governments, large corporations and businesses, health care systems around the world, millions of global consumers.

Why is it being demanded?

To cope with the ever-increasing levels of stress in the workplace, stress due to disabling diseases, stress due to spiraling social and economic changes.

Potential outcome?

All world governments especially America are willing to pay handsome remunerations for persons with these skills and accordingly these careers hold the keys to very bright futures for both personal and financial success.

PROFESSIONAL CAREERS

Type of career/skill?

Personal financial planning assistants and personal income tax preparation accountants.

Who is demanding it?

Seniors and aging baby boomers, special needs persons, entrepreneurs and small businesses, large financial institutions and accounting firms.

Why is it being demanded?

Financial institutions and accounting firms are seeking these professionals to help them offer those services that

would cater more to those types of consumers listed above
while those consumers are seeking to grow and safeguard
their investments and they are looking for personalized
services from these types of professionals.

Potential outcome?

The North American picture is very bright for these types
of careers and it can potentially offer you great financial
security as more and more consumers seek these types of
services.

Type of career/skill?

Architects.

Who is demanding it?

America, other world governments, medium and large
businesses, airports, railways, hotels, movie complexes,
airlines, cruise lines, restaurants, amusement facilities,
vacation spots, so many more.

Why is it being demanded?

With a rapidly aging population, and Section 508
legislation that is an American law, many are scrambling to
make their buildings more accessible to all.

Potential outcome?

The prospects for anyone choosing this career are
extremely promising and lucrative. Financial success is
practically guaranteed for as long as it is necessary. Almost
any and everyone are looking for persons with this skill.

Type of career/skill?

Travel agents and tour guides.

Who is demanding it?

The American government, other world governments,
seniors and aging baby boomers, special needs persons,
families with kids, large travel agencies, cruise lines, tour
companies.

Why is it being demanded?

More and more consumers and governments are
demanding more personalized, accessible, and customized
services from the travel industry.

Potential outcome?

The potential for financial success is very real. Untapped wealth is yours for the taking and prospects and opportunities will only increase with time. Job opportunities abound both in and out of North America.

Type of career/skill?

Fashion designers to design clothes for a rapidly aging population.

Who is demanding it?

Aging baby boomers, seniors, fashion outlets, fashion design houses, department stores and boutiques.

Why is it being demanded?

To meet the needs and satisfy the preferences of a rapidly aging population.

Note: Calvin Klein and the Gap chain have already started to cater to these demands.

Potential outcome?

Limitless if you can step up to these demands. The potential for endless income and job opportunities exist any and everywhere.

Type of career/skill?

Cosmetologists and beauticians.

Who is demanding it?

Seniors and aging baby boomers, young professionals, teenagers, middle-aged persons, and millions of others.

Why is it being demanded?

Potential outcome?

Absolutely mind-boggling! Both personal and financial success is awaiting you and the opportunities to cash in on untapped wealth are very real. Job opportunities are boundless.

Type of career/skill?

Data recovery specialists.

Who is demanding it?

All world governments, businesses and organizations of all sizes, Internet businesses of every denomination, individuals, institutions of learning.

Why is it being demanded?

To deal with the ever increasing incidents of loss of data on hard drives, other computer devices, and hand held devices.

Potential outcome?

Absolutely phenomenal. The opportunity to enjoy a career that is filled with personal satisfaction and loaded with financial success is yours if you want it. Job opportunities abound in almost any IT department of any business, or in any government department.

Type of career/skill?

internet security specialists.

Who is demanding it?

World governments, businesses and organizations of all sizes, Internet businesses of every denomination, individuals, institutions of learning.

Why is it being demanded?

World governments, businesses, and individuals are all terribly concerned about Internet security.

Potential outcome?

Limitless for those who are qualified to provide the right type of Internet security. Financial wealth is unheralded and the opportunity to tap into untapped wealth is right around the corner.

Type of career/skill?

Computer trainers and instructors.

Who is demanding it?

Seniors, aging baby boomers, special needs persons, millions of others.

Why is it being demanded?

More and more persons are clamoring to learn how to work and surf on the Internet.

Potential outcome?

A very bright future with lots of financial stability and highly paid jobs both in and out of North America.

Type of career/skill?

Translators, language coaches, and interpreters.

Who is demanding it?

World governments, international businesses and corporations, organizations, individuals.

Why is it being demanded?

To keep up with the spiraling demands from the growth of international trade.

Potential outcome?

The potential for financial success is very bright and will only continue to look brighter with time. Job opportunities abound everywhere.

Type of career/skill?

Transcribers and virtual assistants.

Who is demanding it?

World governments, business and organizations of all sizes, lawyers, doctors, health care systems, institutions of learning, individuals.

Why is it being demanded?

To meet the ballooning demands for accuracy and efficiency of minute taking and note taking during conferences, meetings, seminars, presentations, interviews, and other related types of circumstances.

Potential outcome?

The potential for financial security is growing at a very steady rate and will continue to do so as time marches on. Jobs can be found both in and out of North America and can be done from home, from the office, and from practically anywhere.

Type of career/skill?

Accessibility consultants.

Who is demanding it?

World governments especially America, businesses of all sizes, the travel and entertainment industry, airlines, airports, cruise lines, railways, subways, cities, states, agencies.

Why is it being demanded?

To meet the needs of seniors, aging baby boomers, special needs persons.

Potential outcome?

America and her sister world governments are willing to pay big bucks for persons who are highly skilled in this area. The potential to tap into untapped wealth is the sky and job opportunities are springing up everywhere.

It is our honest belief that many of the types of careers and skills that we have discussed in this chapter can be pursued by almost everyone. There are career opportunities for:

- the young professional
- the mature professional
- those soon to retire
- the retiree
- the woman on maternity leave
- the housewife or mother at home
- the student looking for a part-time job
- the college and/or university graduate
- the high school student

These careers and skills can be pursued as:

- fulltime employment
- part-time employment
- a second career

CHAPTER SUMMARY

In this chapter we have given you a list of careers and skills that many business experts are saying will be in demand for a very long time. The American government agrees with this viewpoint, as do the World Health Organization, big businesses and corporations, the United Nations, other world governments, and hundreds of millions of consumers.

These careers and skills are poised to help you discover untapped wealth in many hidden, niche, and undiscovered markets. They are safe careers that will allow you to control your own destiny, find tremendous personal satisfaction, and enjoy the life styles of your choice. They are careers that many world governments, including America, are willing and ready to pay handsomely for. They are the careers that big businesses and corporations are scrambling to offer to existing and potential employees.

Our lists are by no means complete, but we are sure that our suggestions will help you to identify many more.

PART FIVE
USEFUL INFORMATION

In this final section we will use chapter eight to provide a wrap up of our book and in chapter nine we will share some success stories with you. These success stories are from some of our clients who were good enough to allow us to do so.

CHAPTER EIGHT
WRAP UP

We hope by now we have convinced you that you do not need to depend on get-rich-quick schemes in order to secure your financial future. There are too many opportunities out there that are safe and sound enough for you to avoid those awful infomercials, fast talking salesmen, and enticing phone calls. There is absolutely no need for you to put yourself at risk of separating yourself from your hard earned money because there are concrete alternatives for you to follow.

We have proven that our strategies have worked and will continue to work for a very long time. We have shown you how to control your own destiny instead of leaving it in the hands of others. We have introduced you to four of the safest global markets that you will ever find, successful businesses that you can either invest in or set up for yourselves, and careers that you can pursue if you are truly serious about tapping into untapped wealth.

Our strategies are based on the principles of logic and common sense and operate on the **RULE** concept.

- **R** stands for read about your perspective markets and their consumers.

- **U** stands for understand your info.
- **L** stands for learn the details about everything pertaining to your markets and their consumers.
- **E** stands for execute the plan.

In chapter one we described the most important dimensions of four of the safest and most resilient global markets that you will ever find and we provided you with questions that you could use to test yourself to see if you would be willing and ready to take the big step to discovering untapped wealth. In chapters two to five inclusive we described each of the four global markets and gave you self-evaluation questions to help you determine your readiness to enter these markets. In chapter six we presented you with a list of best businesses for success and in chapter seven we presented you with a list of most suitable careers and skills.

Many of our clients continuously use our book to help them discover untapped wealth in untapped markets. They use chapters six and seven to help them generate additional ideas for successful businesses and careers. We hope that the stories told in chapter nine will motivate you to find your very own niche where you would be able to discover and carve out your very own reservoir of untapped wealth.

We have used this book to help many different types of clients ranging from:

- the high school student to the retiree
- the college and/or university student to the mom on maternity leave
- the housewife to the young professional
- the matured professional to the pre retiree
- the entrepreneur to the small business owner

Some parents have even been using our strategies to help launch the entrepreneurial careers of their teens, taking our ideas to generate businesses for them. We can give you some examples of parents who have helped their youngsters to get started and we should add here that it is never too early to think about helping your youngsters to launch their entrepreneurial careers.

With the help of his parents, one teen has been able to start his very own dog walking service. Another teenaged girl started her personal shopping service whereby she helped seniors in her area to go grocery shopping. She has expanded this enterprise to taking them for walks. Another pre-teen boy has been helped by his parents to start a pet sitting service, and yet another has launched his own car wash service.

We have also helped several housewives and moms to find their niches by becoming home business entrepreneurs. Some have ventured into the virtual assistant business, others have gone into the translation business, while others have used their existing skills to bring their hairdressing services to the homes of their customers. Some more adventurous clients have opened up catering services whereby they offer their services to seniors and aging baby boomers, while others have opened up their houses to offer social evenings to seniors, single mothers, and so on.

When looking for new markets and new niches you should keep in mind the following:

o   Make sure that you are very clear as to the product or service that you wish to offer.

o   Start small and don't try to take in the big picture all at once. Break it down into manageable pieces.

o   Ensure that you have the skills that are required to sell your product and/or service.

o   Ensure that there is a demand for what you wish to sell.

o   Make sure that demand is more than supply.

o   Get to know your targeted consumers.

o   Make sure that you are selling what they want to buy and not what you want to sell.

o   Listen to what your consumers are demanding.

o   Map out a business plan before you do anything else.

o   Be very sure that you really want to venture into something new. Too many persons fail because they are not quite ready to take this big step.

o   Decide if you want to be fulltime, part-time, or whether you want to go into a side business.

One of the most common pitfalls we have seen is the one where so many businesses and individuals try to customize the demands and needs of their consumers in order to suit the product and/or service that they are selling. We have already mentioned this but we feel that it is important enough for us to give you just a few examples, because avoiding this pitfall can mean the difference between success and failure. We have actually had to rescue some of our clients from this pitfall before it was too late and luckily they have been able to get back on the right track.

Here are some important "Don'ts" for you to remember.

- Don't ever assume that certain consumers will buy a certain product simply because it is being sold at an affordable price.
- Don't ever assume that they would want to purchase a certain type of service because it is cheap.
- Don't ever assume that they would want to buy something because it's the thing to buy at the present time.
- Don't ever assume that a certain type of business can work in a big city because it has worked in a small town.
- Don't ever start a business before you have developed a sound business plan.
- Don't ever start a business before determining the needs of your targeted consumers.

In order to determine whether or not a potential market can yield potential and continuous income you need to consider the following:

- Is consumer growth presently on an upward trend?
- If so, is it expected to continue in this way for at least the next five to 10 years?
- Is demand presently ahead of supply?
- If so, how long has it been like this?

- Is it expected to continue like this for at least the next five to 10 years?
- Does the market exist only in America?
- Does it exist outside of America?
- Is it a global market?
- Is the market expected to exist for at least the next five to 10 years?

We have some final reminders for you for you to keep in mind:

A consumer can belong to more than one market, like the senior who is an Internet user, and also a diabetic. Even if a market is crowded with competitors it is always possible to find that corner that is not very crowded. Think of the skating rink concept. Remember the "RULE" concept. **R**ead, **U**nderstand, **L**earn, and **E**xecute.

If you have an Internet based business, remember the "Ziplock" concept. The more accessible you design your websites to be, the more customers you will attract. In addition, you will be able to reduce both your internal and external costs, increase your customer base and most of all, increase your revenues.

If you run a regular type of business take care to ensure that your business location is accessible and conveniently located and that the layout of your displays and facilities can be easily accessed by all of your consumers. The more accessible you make your business location, your displays and facilities, the greater the potential for you to attract many new customers as well as increase your revenues.

Finally, please do not forget to use the **WWWH** concept. The inclusion or omission of this very important little strategy can go a long way toward making or breaking the success of your business venture. Just ask some of our clients.

W: for who is demanding it.

W: for what is being demanded.

Why: for why it is being demanded.

H: for how to fulfill the demand.

That's it! Turn next to chapter nine for some real life business cases.

CHAPTER SUMMARY

In this chapter we have summarized the main points covered in our book. We revisited the four largest global markets and told you which chapters to read.

Chapter two describes one of the largest global markets that you will ever find. This market is one of the most financially influential that you will ever see and both its demands and consumer growth are expected to grow for a life time as growth is being fueled by a rapidly aging population as well as disabling diseases.

Chapter three describes a market where consumers are pushing their demands to lofty heights and all world governments are extremely concerned.

Chapter four describes a market that is expected to grow both in consumer size and demand for as long as technology continues to evolve and for as long as the Internet is around.

Chapter five describes a market made up of hundreds of millions of global users who are seeking services and products in order to keep up with the evolution of international trade.

Chapters six and seven contain useful information on best businesses and careers for success.

CHAPTER NINE
BUSINESS CASES

In this final chapter we are going to tell you about some clients of ours who have found financial success. In order to preserve the status of consultant client confidentiality, we will give fictitious names to the clients. However, everything else is authentic. It is our hope that these real business cases will inspire you to seek your very own financial success and that you will find them useful models to follow. We have chosen these particular cases as they all relate to the material covered in this book.

CASE ONE

About three years ago Mark Jansen approached us because he felt that we could help him to improve his revenues. Mark was the owner of a travel agency in Boston and at that time he was not doing too badly. However he wanted to know what he could do in order to attract still more customers and increase his revenues.

The first order of business for us was to create a profile that we would use to determine how to go about meeting Mark's objectives. Before we started we told him that his objectives of increasing his customer and revenue bases could not be met unless we had some specific information. He did not hesitate to give whatever was asked for.

We spent some time with Mark in order to create the profile and at the end of it all, we came up with the following. The travel agency was located on the second floor of a nice new building in down town Boston. Although the offices were well laid out the agency was not visible to passersby on the street. The staff was very friendly and eager to help. We spent some time observing them at work as they handled customers both on the phone and face to face and were quite pleased with their customer support.

Most of the travel agency's business was being generated by the following types of customers:

people booking trips to Disney World in Florida, persons going on ski trips to Colorado, and vacationers going on trips to the Caribbean. There were also a few vacationers to Europe.

Further analysis on our part revealed that Mark's travel agency experienced slumps between the months of mid November to end of April and also between May to mid November. At these times, the agency had to work very hard in order to keep busy. This they did by attracting some business travelers and a few customers who booked cruises during this time.

Most of Mark's customers were either families with young or teenaged kids, or couples ranging in age from their mid 20s to their late 40s. His advertising was done mainly through newspaper ads, brochures, and by word of mouth. At the time of our consulting, the travel agency did not have any type of Internet presence, and its business hours were from 9 am to 5 pm Monday to Friday.

After studying the facts and figures, and carrying out the normal marketing analysis, we came up with a game plan, which included a budget. Everything was discussed with Mark and at the end of some lengthy meetings we presented him with a detailed proposal as to what he could do in order to increase both his customer and revenue bases.

The following is a summary of our proposal.

We would work to ensure that the agency would be kept busy all year round instead of only being busy for about six months. We would focus on targeting a much wider variety of customers. We would use the Internet as a means of advertising. We would expand the business hours and the types of services that the agency offered.

This is how the picture looked after everything was sorted out, the budgets for change approved, and after the first six months of operation under the new system.

Mark's travel agency had business hours Monday to Friday from 8 am to 8 pm, and Saturdays from 9 am to 6 pm. The travel agency could be reached either by phone or by email. Advertising was being done through newspaper ads, brochures, magazines, and a newly created website.

Mark was advertising mainly in those magazines that were being read by retirees and pre retirees, and travel magazines. He was able to erect a very appealing neon sign at street level that easily caught the eye of passersby, and his website was being used most effectively.

Let us take a brief moment to comment on Mark's website. The URL for the website was very carefully chosen and reflected the type of business that was being advertised. As well, the website was registered with several search engines and the use of strategic key words was employed.

On the website, surfers could read about the services of the agency, its hours of business, send emails of enquiry to the travel agency, and gain very useful information on many of the more popular vacation hot spots around the world. In addition, the website was written in simple and easy to read English and even had equivalent links in Spanish.

This website contained a very interesting and somewhat unique feature. If a customer was unsure about what type of vacation they wanted to go on, they could go to a link called "vacation planner" that prompted them for information like this.

Enter the type of vacation you wish to have. Example: a cruise, a trip by train, or a trip by plane. The choice entered would determine which page would be next displayed.

There were separate links for cruises, train trips, and destinations by air. The questions for each link were very similar. Below is a sample of these questions.

- Enter your first three choices for a vacation spot.
- Enter the length of time for your intended vacation.
- Enter the desired month for your vacation.
- If possible, enter the approximate start date (mm/dd/yy)
- How many adults are in the party?
- How many children are the party?
- List the ages of any children.
- How many seniors are there in the party?

Based on these questions three possible vacation packages would then be presented along with costs and the best time to travel. A customer could then do any of the following: Choose one of the packages, send an email to the travel agency with further questions, or simply download the information for future reference.

We encouraged Mark to offer cruise packages and special tours for seniors and families that included door to door service, help with obtaining visas if needed, and help with baggage at airports and train stations. We also proposed that the agency

sell simple guides in some of the more popular languages and that the agency provide their traveling customers with useful compilations of information about the customs and culture of their destination at no cost. These compilations could be gathered via the Internet.

Within six months of the implementation of our proposals Mark started to see a noticeable change in his business fortunes. At the end of the first year his revenues increased by 30% and the number of enquiries was picking up nicely. He was very pleased with his website advertising and the numbers of visitors to his website was just incredible. He even placed newsletters on his website which visitors could subscribe to at no cost.

At the end of the second year revenues had increased by a further 50% and by the end of the third year Mark's revenues had increased by over 100% from the first day that we had met him. Today, Mark is earning a very healthy six figure income thanks to a team effort that includes the implementation of our strategies, his business savvy and hard work on the part of both him and his growing staff.

(The following chart illustrates the growth Mark experienced in his revenue after consultation with the authors of this book, business consultants for Sterling Creations.)

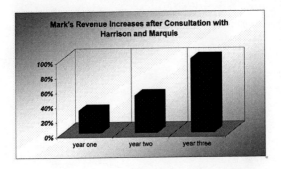

CASE TWO

Melissa Carpenter is probably one of our favorite clients because she impressed us so much with her spunk and willingness to try something new. When we were first introduced to Melissa, she had just been laid off from a very well paying job at a large computer company in California and she was at a bit of a loss as to what she should do next.

Melissa approached us to help her find her next career. After a few meetings with her, we determined that she had saved well and now she was willing to spend up to about fifty thousand dollars in order to launch her next career. She possessed excellent sales and Internet skills and she possessed a very deep interest in the health care industry. Melissa, coincidentally, was also a diabetic.

We got to work on using her profile in order to develop a strategy for her and upon completion of the analysis; we presented her with the following proposal.

We proposed that Melissa go into an Internet based business where she would set up an online store primarily for diabetics. The store would also be a place where health conscious consumers could buy products. Melissa was elated because she could use her knowledge as a diabetic in order to help others. Moreover, she could do most of the work herself to set up her own website.

She chose a unique URL for her website, developed an eye-catching but elegantly simple set of web pages, and registered with several search engines using the appropriate key words in order to attract her customers. She too used newsletters, which could be subscribed to for free, in order to attract the attention of visitors. Melissa even skillfully employed the services of pay per click companies.

The types of products and services that Melissa offered included

door-to-door delivery of products such as kits, jams, chocolates, and other types of sugar free products for the diabetic consumer. These products were attractively priced and quick delivery was guaranteed. Customers could order by email or by phoning a 1-800 toll free number and she could be reached on a 24/7 basis, including public holidays.

Melissa also sold books on healthy diets for diabetics and the health conscious consumer, exercise videos, and some products for the visually impaired. She secured her supplies by entering into arrangements with various stores and vendors to sell their products on the Internet.

Melissa worked untiringly to make her venture a success and eight months after opening her doors for business she began to see her labor paying off. She runs her business out of her house and this helps to cut down on her operating costs. Her skills enable her to do most of her own work but she has had to employ an assistant to help her cope with the growing business. She is even contemplating writing a book and we have advised her that she can use this book in order to enhance the promotion of her website.

One year after she started her business, Melissa was earning around $75,000.00 (seventy-five thousand dollars) after taxes, and after two years she had happily attained the six-figure mark. She also hired a second assistant and has plans to expand her product line.

We have worked hard to ensure that her website is easy to navigate, is written in easy to understand language, and that it is relatively easy to order products. We have also advised her to include equivalent links in Spanish and she has promised to give careful consideration to the suggestion. On our advice, she has placed great importance on ensuring that her website can be accessed by visually impaired persons, as so many diabetics are also visually impaired.

We continue to work with Melissa on an ongoing basis and our latest project is for her to write books where she can impart her knowledge and expertise. Plans are in the works for her to compile a book on best eating choices for the diabetic and the health conscious consumer, healthy recipes, and healthy living for diabetics. What we enjoy the most with this client is that she is constantly coming up with ideas to improve and enhance her business, just as we continually advise all our clients to do.

We firmly believe that when one project is complete you have to move on to the next one in order to enhance and continue the process of revenue generation. In Melissa's case, she is constantly building on her business by finding ways to offer products and services that are related to each other in some way or other.

She is using her knowledge and skills to do just that. She is selling products that relate to each other. For example, the diabetic consumer needs kits, diet books, and those types of sugar free products that she is selling. She has expanded her product line to include the health conscious consumer who is also constantly looking for those healthy eating diet books and the exercise videos. These books and videos are big sellers. We have even suggested to Melissa that she think about selling exercise suits.

CASE THREE

Now we are going to turn our attention to two clients whom we have helped to become entrepreneurs, by using their language skills. First we have Nicholas Gregory who approached us a few years ago after he had graduated from college. Nicholas, (Nick from now on) was referred to us by his mother who had been a friend of ours at University.

Nick was living in Chicago at the time, where he had obtained a double major degree in Japanese and economics. Upon his graduation he spent six very frustrating months looking for jobs, had several fruitless interviews, and was beginning to get discouraged. After meeting with him and determining that he possessed a very interesting background, we got to work to build a profile for him and to create a strategy.

The final picture looked like this. We used Nick's skills to develop a profile of someone who possessed the qualifications to be a consultant for those Japanese businessmen seeking to expand their commerce in North America and Britain. We told Nick that he could use his degree to become a very important business consultant. A combination of Japanese and Economics could be turned into a very potent and unique consultant's weapon when it came to doing business with the Japanese.

We worked with Nick to implement the strategy. Together we designed a formidable information package and began by advertising it through the Internet. We decided that it would be more economic and cost effective for Nick to start with his own website and then expand his advertising through other channels.

We developed a highly professional website with well-written content to describe Nick's services. The website contained a sales letter with accolades from his college and university professors, and supervisors and managers that he had worked with during his summer and part-time jobs. These accolades talked about his experiences and the clients for whom he had worked.

In addition, we used the appropriate key words to set him up with all of the popular search engines and employed newsletters, which talked about the benefits of increasing business relations between the United States and Japan.

We developed a strategy for Nick to use his website so that he could advertise himself like this.

"A business consultant specializing in American/Japanese relations can help you to better understand the socio economic issues of both America and Japan. This consultant can help you to enrich your business relations and give you a huge advantage over your competition by giving you customized courses on the culture, language, and customs of both America and Japan. If you need to practice your language skills or you wish to receive individual coaching on how to carry out an interview or be interviewed in either English or Japanese, then you have come to the right place."

For the first three months after launching his website, Nick did not get much response and naturally he started to become despondent but a breakthrough came during the fourth month. Nick was having lunch in a Japanese restaurant one day and while eating with some friends he noticed some Japanese people having lunch nearby. On an impulse he left his eating companions and wandered over to the table where the others were dining. To summarize, he introduced himself, a conversation began, and by the end of it all he had given out several of his business cards.

A week later he received an email from someone in Japan enquiring about his services. Two weeks and several emails later Nick landed his first consulting contract. Though it was only a five thousand dollar contract it was the beginning for our client.

By the end of the first year Nick had earned about thirty thousand dollars in consulting contracts and by the end of the second year his income had reached seventy thousand dollars.

Three years after that first meeting with Nick, he is doing exceedingly well and has needed to hire an administrative assistant. He is slowly building a name for himself and the demand for his type of expertise is steadily growing. His income has just passed the six figure mark and we expect that as American/Japanese relations continue to blossom, so too will Nick's income.

(The following chart illustrates the growth Nick experienced in his revenue after consultation with the authors of this book, business consultants for Sterling Creations.)

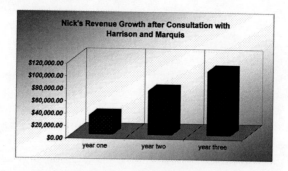

In addition to his website on the Internet, we have developed an advertising strategy for Nick whereby he has joined several networking associations and uses them to spread the word about his services. He has also joined several associations that deal specifically with American/Japanese business and cultural activities. All of these channels are proving most useful in helping to create more business for Nick. He has had to change his business location twice during the first three years because of his growing consulting services and he has also had to hire some additional staff to help him.

Now it is time for use to introduce our next client to you. Her name is Amanda Martinez and we met her five years ago at a seminar in Miami. The seminar was held for those who were looking to prolong their careers after retirement and we were both guest speakers. Amanda approached us during one of the intermissions and as with our other clients we held several meetings with her before presenting her with a strategy.

We used these meetings to build a profile for Amanda and after our analysis we came up with a strategy. Her profile looked like this:

Amanda had just retired as a schoolteacher. For 25 years she had taught Spanish to high school students and so she was fluent in both Spanish and English.

Amanda did not want to acquire too many new skills in order to launch her after retirement career but to build instead on her present skills and experience. She was a housewife with grown kids and had lots of time on her hands to venture into new projects. However, she did not want to spend too much money on launching her new career because she had other financial commitments to deal with.

With her pre-requisites in mind and a budget of ten thousand dollars to work with, we developed a strategy for Amanda.

First, Amanda took a six-month translation course from a New York based university through the Internet from the comfort of her home. At the end of this course she was certified as a bilingual translator to translate documents, brochures, and reports from English to Spanish and visa versa.

Next we developed a website that advertised her translation services. The services she offered included the following: translation of documents, brochures, and reports from English to Spanish and Spanish to English; translation of web pages from English to Spanish and Spanish to English;

and private tutoring of Spanish speaking students to improve their English speaking skills, and English-speaking students to improve their Spanish speaking skills.

We developed a sales letter that promoted these services and described Amanda's skills as a bilingual teacher of English and Spanish with many years of experience. The sales letter also contained accolades from some of her former students, fellow teachers, and persons with whom she had worked while she was volunteering as a teacher in a Spanish community. In addition to our sales letter, we registered the website using the appropriate key words with the more popular search engines.

The website also contained a link that allowed a potential customer to enter their requirements for translation. For example the customer could enter their first and last names, email address, type of document, number of words, and how soon they wished to have their work completed. Amanda would then evaluate each order and send back an estimate to the potential customer.

In order to push her marketing along, we advised Amanda to print business cards and simple brochures in both English and Spanish and she distributed these to high schools, associations for Spanish Americans, and various government departments dealing with the migration of Spanish speaking persons to America.

In order to cut down on costs, Amanda personally took her brochures to these places, made personal visits to the schools and associations, and did most of her own phone calls. Amanda also started out by working from home.

One year after she opened her doors for business, Amanda had a very meager income of five thousand dollars so you can see that she had not yet recovered her initial investment of ten thousand dollars plus our consulting fee. Naturally Amanda was very disappointed and ready to give up but with a bit of convincing from us and more hard work and determination on her part, she struggled on.

Her efforts began to really pay off around the fourth month into the second year. She began to receive phone calls from students seeking tutoring help, emails requesting translations.

At the end of the second year and eight months after her turning point, Amanda had a gross income of thirty-five thousand dollars and she was quite happy that she had decided to stick with her new career. She was now operating in the black! Three years after she first opened her doors for business Amanda had more than doubled her income and at that time she decided to rent a small office close to her home in order to meet the increasing demands for her services. She too has had to hire an assistant to help with the growing business.

OTHER CLIENTS

We will close this chapter by giving you two more examples of clients. These examples are much briefer than those above, but still as relevant. They are clients using their existing skills in order to tap into the untapped markets discussed throughout this book.

Hairdresser on call

First, meet Cathy Mitzky who is using her hairdressing skills to tap into the untapped markets. Cathy has set herself up as a hairdresser on call. She uses a van that contains all of her equipment and tools of the trade and she advertises herself to hospitals, homes for seniors, and large corporations.

We first met Cathy soon after she had graduated from hairdressing school in New York and it is a project that we developed together. She is on call anytime of the day from 8 am to 8 pm and works Mondays to Fridays.

Cathy is kept extremely busy but she enjoys her work immensely. Her costs are being kept to a minimum and on average she makes around seventy thousand dollars annually. Three years after she first started we decided that it was time for her to expand her business and she has been fortunate to find a partner who also uses a van to work as a hairdresser on call. Her income has more than doubled since she took on her partner.

Bed and breakfast

Mr. and Mrs. Chad Corseau in New Jersey approached us a few years ago because they wanted help to market their bed and breakfast facility and were looking for a way to make their B&B unique.

We decided to discuss those famous untapped markets with them and after some discussion we decided that they would work to advertise their B&B as a place where our Seniors could find all the facilities and comforts to suit their needs. There were even facilities to accommodate our special needs persons.

This meant that they had to make their B&B accessible in order to meet the needs of persons in wheel chairs, and with walkers, and that they also had to install ramps and widen doorways. They needed to reconfigure their light switches in order to accommodate persons in wheel chairs, and they even equipped their bathrooms to better meet the new clientele.

Mr. and Mrs. Corseau changed the colors of their doors to accommodate those with low vision, and placed the door handles and knobs in strategic positions so that all of their perspective clients could be accommodated. The handles and knobs were uniquely designed to meet the needs of those clients who would have difficulty in grasping them.

Chad used his skills as an architect to do most of his renovations but he had to spend money to hire skilled labor to complete the rest of this huge project. Fortunately for the Corseaus they had the financial resources to undertake this venture.

We advertised the Corseau B&B on the Internet, and through the various tourist channels in New Jersey. Chad and Michelle Corseau did not have to wait very long before starting to take in new clients. The first year brought them an income of about fifty thousand dollars but by the second year they had crossed that six-figure mark. After three years they are servicing clients from as far away as Europe and Asia.

CHAPTER SUMMARY

We hope that the cases presented in this chapter will help to convince you that there are indeed untapped markets needing your input. These markets are very much alive, have real and rapidly increasing demands, and are just waiting for you.

You can certainly use your existing skills to reap your financial rewards or obtain new skills in order to seek your fortunes. The success stories presented in this chapter are all those of persons who were determined to work hard in order to accomplish their goals. They have given their all to their various ventures, and were all bound and determined to succeed.

We have had some clients along the way who have not been as successful as those introduced to you in this chapter. Their lack of success was most likely due to their not being dedicated enough to their dreams of success. Success is made up of a dream that can only turn into reality if you dedicate yourself to hard work, endless patience, and tireless determination.

All of the clients that you have met in this chapter were very determined in their own way to find their financial success.

They either used their existing skills or acquired new ones in order to make it work for them. It is our sincere hope that you too can benefit from these cases.

If you have any questions, please write to us at: info@untappedwalth.com.

211715

Made in the USA